THE PUZZLE

The Individual In Education

THE PUZZLE

The Individual In Education

Daniel J. Dyman, Ed.D.

Order this book online at www.trafford.com/08-1003
or email orders@trafford.com

Most Trafford titles are also available at major online book retailers.

Note for Librarians: A cataloguing record for this book is available from Library and Archives Canada at www.collectionscanada.ca/amicus/index-e.html

ISBN: 978-1-4251-8484-1

We at Trafford believe that it is the responsibility of us all, as both individuals and corporations, to make choices that are environmentally and socially sound. You, in turn, are supporting this responsible conduct each time you purchase a Trafford book, or make use of our publishing services. To find out how you are helping, please visit www.trafford.com/responsiblepublishing.html

Our mission is to efficiently provide the world's finest, most comprehensive book publishing service, enabling every author to experience success. To find out how to publish your book, your way, and have it available worldwide, visit us online at www.trafford.com/10510

www.trafford.com

North America & international
toll-free: 1 888 232 4444 (USA & Canada)
phone: 250 383 6864 • fax: 250 383 6804 • email: info@trafford.com

The United Kingdom & Europe
phone: +44 (0)1865 487 395 • local rate: 0845 230 9601
facsimile: +44 (0)1865 481 507 • email: info.uk@trafford.com

10 9 8 7 6 5 4 3 2 1

TO MY FATHER

for all that I have to give

ACKNOWLEDGEMENTS

Alissa

Betsy

Christy

Esme

Hopey

Jan

Jimmy

John

Lindsay

Paul

Rachel

Susan

Tylor

1

The most important entity in education is the student. While "No Child Left Behind" may seem to be a worthy directive signed into law on January 8, 2002, perhaps because of it, many or even all children are being left behind. In its wake, countless well intending though self-limiting interferences along with the recently set into place state standards are restricting the potential of schools and their teachers. Consequently, while some test scores may show a measure of improvement, students nonetheless, are more at risk.

The progress welcomed as it is out of some perceived need may be only a product of regulation. Rather than what might have been, any of the results as they are, had been determined by self-preserving but system restricting manipulation. The recent attempts that were proposed to force schools to do better are in effect oppressive and likely will cause a regression in substantive performance. In all things, free enterprise leads to better outcomes.

How is it that before the last few generations the children apparently did not get left behind? Could there have been issues that went without attention, had been unnoticed, or were ignored?

Regardless, recent surveys of academic performance confirm that the children of the United States as they approach graduation into the marketplace have fallen behind in language skills and mathematics as well as in science, areas of relevance that affect global participation. At least one survey of performance confirms that while elementary school age children of the United States lead in performance, they are lagging by the time they matriculate into high school, ranked as low as twenty-sixth among the so-called advanced nations.

Does that suggest anything? What is happening during those few years? What might be the cause of this noted shortfall? How significant are these evaluations? Are any of these gathered insights at least in some way selective? Are any of these discernments applicable developed more out of an interest to maintain a righteous competitive edge, a proclivity to be in front, or out of a real desire to be individually as good as good can be?

Only the latter is a pursuit of merit.

After all, our comparative lackluster worldwide rank may be only of secondary importance and that the prescription for honorable improvement is within our grasp only to be teased apart from among many ordered impositions, rules, and regulations.

Given the bottom line, unless in some way deprived during pre-birth development, children are born with inherent curiosity. They exhibit the fundamental inclination for learning but along the way for some this inherent quality apparently yields to no doubt a variety of subconscious prohibitive perceptions and assumptions.

Enthusiasm for learning gradually fades away. Fortunately among these now older school age individuals most are at least politely submissive to the classroom structures. They try. While acceptable, within this group many exhibit a cooperative behavior only because they are driven by a specific praiseworthy motivation or even an externally imposed incentive. On the other hand, some are outwardly disruptive and deliberately resistant to the processes of commonplace teaching that can result in learning. Their justifications are more than they are in number pouting over supposed losses or coping with exceedingly complex hardships.

From this broadened perspective, the school processes and their impact upon an assortment of individual needs now require careful examination. Arriving at new realizations could positively change the interactive teaching/learning practices and yield compelling results that are beyond comparison.

How does the system of education get fixed so that self-fulfilling individual outcomes are attained? That is the puzzle.

Quite a few years ago, with a liberal arts degree in hand and a teaching assignment in a parochial school, my career in education began. The young people welcomed me and appreciated what together we were able to accomplish. Perhaps I learned more than the students.

On that foundation, I have come to realize that those in the profession need to be given the responsibility for its success and they need to become learners themselves so that quickly they can make assessments and appropriately implement the needed adjustments enabling the next generation to be personally accomplished as well as marketplace competitive and productive. This can be achieved if the prescribed learning is attainable and success is possible as well as rewarding. However, the external pressures and demands that grow out of authority and an assortment of biases appear to be counterproductive, working against the all enabling teaching and learning enterprises.

More time in class, additional pages to cover with homework assignments, plus more tests are not producing the incentives for learning. More of "this and that" may be resulting in less of everything. In the teaching and learning enterprise, it has to be quality over volume predicated upon a ration of sensibility. As has been well established success grows from a nurturing environment rather than from one that can be described as overbearing and perhaps even fearful.

It is time to lighten up. The demands for results that are placed upon teachers and students are ever increasing. A camel might respond after a full load, "Every straw does count." Nonetheless, the questionable notion prevails that if schools are to measure up, if student performance levels are to improve, then the bar must be constantly raised. Subjected to these widespread notions some students will persist and prevail, many others can be expected to give up and quit. Significantly, those who have tossed in the towel on education are counted among the coveted averages or are they?

Should any average score be seen as an absolute? Truly, is it not blurred by countless mitigating causes that somehow need to be factored into or out of the result?

Education for all that it is needs to be seen as more than some bottom line average score.

Why not try some other approach looking to achieve some other realistic outcomes?

Albert Einstein is quoted as having said, "Make everything as simple as possible but not simpler."

We learn best when knowledge is structured into relevant concepts, into big ideas. We learn best when we have time to ponder and conceptualize. We learn best when we are filled with wonder.

Schools that are not so enabling fall short in making things understood. In their zealousness these schools mentally beat up their students and psychologically divorce them. These schools then become the "sorters and weeders" of students who prosper only with a toolbox of "factoids," the product of a single resource, the ability to memorize.

Perhaps Benjamin Franklin said it best, "Tell me and I forget. Teach me and I remember. Involve me and I learn."

"Tell me" is often what goes on in a classroom. "Involve me" is not commonplace if it occurs at all. However, students need those who immerse them in the processes derived from creativity that motivate interest and truly lead to learning. Individuality surfaces, diversity emerges, a totality of wholesomeness materializes. The benefits for each and for all will be the best that can be realized.

Is this kind of involvement and immersion possible in the present context and structure of our schools?

Good things as a consequence of learning have to be perceived by the learner. Each recognized achievement can then serve as a step stone to the next higher order accomplishment. But, learners first must be able to achieve. Reasonably falling short in the achievement sequence leads to frustration that dilutes the will and poisons the spirit. Undesirable outcomes are the results determined and compounded by way of confrontation seeded with a morsel if not a spirit of indignation. The continuous raising of the academic challenge coupled to all of its ramifications in effect may be the underlying as well as justifying cause. It is painful to be set aside essentially left behind.

Out of competition, textbook publishers rule. They at least indirectly set the standards. Most if not all of the determined levels for academic achievement are the result of publisher influence inadvertent as that may be. Rather than call upon those who teach and involve students who might have an insight about what should be presented and how it should be taught, publishers fill books with what is perceived as the summation of subject area knowledge. Afterward, they seek approvals from noteworthy figures in the field. The list prefaces the text. Subsequently, the publishers present the "best there is" into the marketplace with each a virtual "look alike" of all the rest.

The "not much to select from" group is basically "more of the same" under a slightly different title. Ultimately, if asked, why "this" or why "that" is included in the curriculum at any grade level, the answer is likely that nobody knows. Search any curriculum area that is to be covered by teachers and learned by students. Justification is limited for both the content to be considered and the extent of its coverage. It seems that publishers have usurped the prerogatives of teachers. They lead the way. However, for best results, the role of the book publishers needs to be altered at least if not reversed.

Classroom teachers who enable positive outcomes need to be involved in curriculum development. Absolutely! They need to be involved. They need to show the way. They need to determine what elements are assigned to various grade levels that may serve as foundations for dependent learning especially at the secondary level.

Yet, with grass roots teachers out of the loop, how can they be responsible and subsequently liable? With an array of non teaching related responsibilities, how is a principal to account for learning and for what is or is not included in any course as well as know the justification should anyone inquire?

Secondary school courses especially should focus on more than a likely by chance blend of "this" with some of "that." If a course is not a prerequisite for some higher level of learning in that subject or some related subject area, it ought to be structured not to give glimpses of esoteric traditions but rather in positive and permitting ways that give students understandings of their world here and now.

Courses need to begin with what is current. Everything included needs to be put into a relevant context, the complexities of a global marketplace.

While on the job at one school, for a parent night open house, the principal imposed upon all teachers the requirement of posting on the chalkboard or marker board the goals of the various courses to which they were assigned. At the time, I was teaching a course in environmental science. While I might have listed many of the goals or the standards that the course addressed, I wrote a paraphrase of a credit card commercial:

Textbook	$89.00
Notebook	2.95
Pencil	.29
To become Good Citizens of Earth	Priceless

A few parents were impressed. One with a musing smile and a supporting nod did stop to say, "Interesting! Interesting."

Indeed, education should concentrate on the development of Good Citizens of Earth, equipped with a reverence for the political and social structures of other cultures, the foundations that allow for the equitable distribution and use of limited resources, and the wherewithal to cope with the impact of day-to-day discoveries from research and exploration. In addition, Good Citizens of Earth would understand the principles of their country, the dynamics of its origin, and its position in relationship with other countries. They would understand the consequences of the aggressive use of resources in a competitive but limited world. They would be marketplace-ready.

Thus, schools need to focus on the enhancement and enrichment of individual inherent talents. Schools should work to develop the four communication skills, reading, writing, speaking, and the overlooked dimension, listening. They should impart knowledge derived from science as well as the operational skills of science. They should develop skills in mathematics especially those that are relevant to everyday interactions. And, they should give insight into the processes of social, political, and economic relations including an understanding of historical development as a foundation for the structures of government operating for the good of all.

Accountability can no longer remain founded on the number of correct responses out of any given number of criteria. Well intended outside influences and demands have to be relinquished to those with the job of teaching. Schools with their teachers must be left with the primary responsibility of getting the job done surely with their success tempered only by the background and environment of their clientele, the students. Success in one environment may be a leap and a bound whereas success in another circumstance may be just a nearly imperceptible nudge.

It may be that rather than focus on relative scores more concern should be directed toward the development of the individual in school. More emphasis should be directed toward the improvement and augmentation of the individual enabling opportunity and access. More importance should be placed upon the development of marketplace-ready individuals. That seems to have overriding significance. That may be the ultimate test. With the world changing rapidly, society and communities need to rethink what is needed. Schools with their teachers need to figure out how that can be accomplished most efficiently and effectively.

What over the years has changed, what during this time has remained the same, and what ideally should be configured for the individual in education?

We have one opportunity to do the tasks of education that are before us. We have in our midst examples of both failure and success. It is our responsibility to tease out what works and implement those teaching methods and techniques with an eye on continuous improvement.

2

"Hello," I said to the clerk when I went to renew my driver's license.

With a smile, she replied, "Have a seat."

While sitting down, I handed over my license.

Giving it a glance, the clerk continued, "You will need a vision test. Place your forehead against the curvature in the optical machine to your right and read line five."

I scooted over in my chair and positioned myself to look into the apparatus as I had been directed. I said, "May I use my glasses?"

In response I heard, "First, try without them."

I looked into the lenses of the instrument. Line five was fuzzy but I felt compelled to try.

I guessed, "five . . . eight . . . six."

Realizing that I was unable to do what was asked of me, I looked away from the apparatus saying, "I am not able to read the numbers but I can read those in line four."

Line four was larger, four sets of numbers with four in each set.

The clerk responded, "No. Try with your glasses."

Using my glasses, I was able to correctly read all of the numbers in line five. With some relief as I looked up toward the clerk I heard, "From now on, you will have to drive with your glasses on. I am going to put a restriction on your license."

"That will be fine," I replied with gratefulness and some relief.

After a picture was taken and a small fee paid, I was issued a renewed driver's license.

As I walked to my car, I thought, "Something is wrong with what just happened. How did the Department of Motor Vehicles come up with this? A disparity exists between the vision test, reading line five, and what I would see on the road as a driver of an automobile."

I took off my glasses. I looked around the parking lot as I continued onward. Clearly, I could see other vehicles even those coming through the aisle as I progressed. I could read the words on the theatre marquee several yards away.

My thinking persisted, "Why should I have to be able to see small illuminated numbers in a vision instrument when in reality as I drive along a road, am I not looking to follow white and yellow lines so as to stay within a traffic lane? Am I not looking for really large signs: yield right of way, stop, merge, and speed limit? Shapes and colors are as important as the words written on the signs. Yes, I am looking for directional arrows, light signals at an intersection or railroad crossing. And, I am looking for oncoming vehicles as well as pedestrians or children who might jump out into the street chasing a ball that had gone astray."

The folks at the DMV were asking me to perform one task with the presumption that several other unrelated tasks were then possible. Abilities were at best indirectly confirmed.

I concluded, "Why was I not given a simulator that tested my prowess on the road?"

Upon returning home, I described my DMV experience to my wife.

I proclaimed, "Certainly, without my glasses, I can see a bicycle rider along the edge of the road, the flashing lights of an approaching emergency vehicle, or a flagman directing traffic around a roadway construction site. Truly, I can see all kinds of other things required for the safe operation of a vehicle. So, why the restriction if I cannot just see a few groups of small numbers?"

In reply, my wife said, "Take it easy. But, driving along the road, you do see signs with letters and numbers. Why are you so adverse to the test?"

"Yes," I argued. "But the lettering is huge. The DMV should test for what is actually needed."

Later that day, my wife and I were en route to a shopping mall. I tested my contention. Without any difficulty even traveling at sixty miles per hour, I was able to read every roadside sign even the smaller mile marker numbers without the aid of my glasses. Importantly, I was able to see clearly details of all dashboard instruments including the speedometer.

I thought, "Are schools operated in a way similar to the DMV? Do schools and of course teachers presume a competency based upon student success on some test instrument that can only indirectly at best validate the presumption of competence? Why?"

Conceivably, careful and thoughtful consideration has not been given to the discrepancy at hand.

My thoughts continued, "How do you judge that? Do you judge it to be irrelevant, inconsequential, or perhaps just nonsense?"

In education, at least I have come to believe that if you think that you are going somewhere, you often end up where you started out. Many of the problems are in fact contingent and interconnected so that figuratively they may appear to be circular. Nonetheless, with some certainty, these presumed circles surround an idea of merit worth discussion.

I am inclined to believe that high school programs are not what they ought to be, that some unheard of but reasonable changes in organization and practices could bring about dramatically better outcomes and that after a lot of data gathering coupled with issues focused dialog action to correct deficiencies is needed. Complaining does not get it done. Figure it out then make it right should be the expeditious course.

In education, with the decades of experience that have accrued, the way has not been resolved. How to consistently get from here to there along the most direct route is undetermined. Constructive alterations in education that could bridge the gap indeed are available but apparently are continuously overlooked or disregarded. Until now, it did not matter.

Is it possible that what goes on in at least some if not most or all high schools and other schools even colleges and universities could be a lot better? Is it possible that established state standards are not all that they could be or ought to be and that state standards intended to improve education, looked to as the ultimate remedy, need to be carefully scrutinized, practically deciphered, for what schools should be accomplishing?

Are the standards more or less like the restriction of having to wear glasses while driving a car because an outcome appears unattained? Is it possible that the imposition of governmental policies will get desired results but accomplish only a portion of what should be achieved by students in the secondary schools because they are not focused clearly upon some elements that really matter? Does merely shooting an arrow necessitate hitting a "bull's eye" let alone the target?

These external pressures may well force an array of unintended consequences. The overall effect will be at best some test for accountability but more than likely it will miss the mark for what truthfully is needed to maintain a rightful place in the global market.

Truly is this nation of youngsters increasingly at risk with the continued loss of academic place among the developed nations of the world as studies have revealed? Is it possible that educators are providing teaching in areas perhaps of little importance while neglecting matters of more or of greater significance? Is it possible that concerns over education will lead the next generation into the workforce with knowledge and skills that do not get the desired economic effects or that might even be considered superfluous in getting the job done? Are those of the next generation getting the right stuff? Is what a person knows of more value than how to know, than how to think?

Why in education is the paramount concern over comparative scores in language and mathematics skills with some deference for science knowledge? Do we want our next generation to prevail in these specific disciplines or do we really want our children to be able to reason sequentially and use the potential of language and mathematics skills to express situations and resolve problems? Do we want know-how in science to serve as a launching pad for understanding the universe and all of its composite elements?

As recognized, much of science as taught is vocabulary set in the context of historical events. Mathematics is presented in the abstract coupled with the mechanics of formula manipulation to get answers. Language skills are developed by way of reading limited to the classics coupled with vocabulary building confined to memorization. Writing is focused upon story telling in prose and verse. Arguably each of these methods and the outcomes generated has some inherent usefulness but the developed capabilities need to be practically extended. Therein is the shortfall.

Is it possible that we are too concerned with this kind of elemental teaching that we lose sight of the purposeful goal?

A story is told of a young lady cooking Thanksgiving dinner for the first time. Before placing the ham into a pot, she cut a chunk from each end. When asked why, she replied, "Because that is what Mother always did."

When confronted with the same question, the mother replied, "Because that is what my mother always did."

Then a perceptive uncle spoke up saying, "But our mother cut off the ends because the only pot that she had was too small to hold the whole ham."

Do schools function similarly? Do they do what they do more out of tradition or habit than because of some well founded substantiated insights? Are those being taught consequently mislead and misguided by these "conventional" methods? Should the school systems become more thoughtful of what they do? Should they not bring into alignment the materials taught and methods used with the needed and desired outcomes and expectations?

A high school junior with remarkable enthusiasm once said to me, "Oh, in the 7th grade, we had to memorize the Periodic Table of Elements."

I replied, "What? Did I understand this correctly? Why?"

Noble as that assignment may seem, those involved in the science education program of that student have come to believe that the memorization of this kind of trivia is a measure of exceptional learning. But, this is not exceptional at all and has little purpose.

If the act of memorization does not improve the ability to remember facts as some studies may have shown, then what is the purpose in memorizing the periodic table other then that it consumes time or that it serves the needs of quiz games that perhaps teach some social skills that are incidental and are not easily measured if that were the purpose? Would it not be better to teach how the periodic table had been constructed and how it is useful and applicable in the domain of chemistry?

That might be too difficult to assess using conventional testing methods. This is reminiscent of the vision test for a driver's license.

Does having the students "regurgitate" the information of the periodic table make the teacher look good or make the students feel proud for having done so as one might feel having surmounted the summit of Mt. Everest?

Certainly, the material readily lends itself to objective criterion based testing. And, objective criterion based testing is the all purpose means by which mostly "factoid" knowledge can be measured without a doubt. It is a lot like reading line five in the vision apparatus used by the DMV.

But, is that not falling short? Are these methods of evaluation excusable?

Henry Ford once sued a newspaper for in print having called him an ignoramus. During the trial, the defense attorney in an attempt to give credence to the allegation asked Mr. Ford a number of questions such as, "What is the date for the beginning of the Civil War? List in order the names of the first ten Presidents of the United States."

Having been able to answer only a few of the questions, Mr. Ford interrupted, "I don't know the answers for many of these questions but if you will give me a few minutes, I'll find somebody who does. I use my brain to think rather than to store up a lot of facts."

Similarly, as a means to show that Albert Einstein was a dunce someone once asked him how many feet were in a mile. Einstein is said to have answered, "I don't know. But, why should I fill my head with information such as that when in just a few minutes I could look up the answer in a reference."

So, why do we ask students to memorize? Why do we ask them to accumulate countless bits of information as if more were better? Why do we ask learners to do any of what goes on in school?

3

Once, while on a field trip, the lead bus on which I had been riding was hit head on by a distracted driver. After all of the clarifications with the police on the scene and the decisions made by administrative staff, many students while appearing uninjured elected to go to nearby hospitals for a check-up, to go home to calm down from their trauma, or to return to school. Needless to say, only a few students returned for classes. Those who did pleaded to play games. With only one third of the students present, the games option was selected as the most viable. By consensus "Thumbs Up and Thumbs Down" was chosen.

As I would learn, this is how the game is played. Except for two or three, all other students would be seated with eyes closed assuming a head down on the desk position with the thumb of one hand extended upward. Those two or three not seated students would walk quietly among the group. Each would push down the thumb of one of those who was seated. Then, those whose thumb had been pushed down would be entitled to guess which of the students had pushed down their thumb. If a student guessed correctly, it would become their turn to walk about the room to push down the thumb of one of their classmates whose face would be buried in their arms and hands. The one found out would become one of those seated.

I thought, "This is too silly?"

Though "Thumbs Up and Thumbs Down" was the preferred game and played by all, upon tiring, those with a different kind of maturity opted in favor of "Hangman," a kind of spelling guess the word game. As students guessed, some laughed others giggled.

With the end of the class period, the students said, "We had fun."

Reflecting upon the experience, non prescribed learning was

taking place. Personalities were enriched and perhaps the wherewithal for teamwork in collaborative environments was being molded. Who is to say what the specific outcomes were? We should try to find out what is the ideal ratio of seriousness to playfulness for every age group. Certainly, unremitting earnestness should not always be required. Play is a mediator for learning.

The field trip students were high school juniors. By their stature and rank, they are considered adolescents, somewhat matured by their array of experiences though limited without question.

By their behavior, is it reasonable to think of them as energetic children, children who must contend with unsettling standards as well as a number of global issues? And, what can be asked about the less matured freshman? How would they have behaved? How would they have responded?

Are those in education really aware of what they are doing and can they justify it? Can they fully explain why they teach what they teach and assess the corresponding learning as they do? Are those in education not cutting off both ends of the ham again and again?

Realistically, what can be expected of high school students? Do they have the wherewithal to handle the stuff of the modern curriculum structured upon demanding state mandated standards? Really can high school students develop a facility for the material represented by these standards? If they can, should they advance into other kinds of programs or to some other level of learning?

Practically, it has been assumed that all students ought to be able to achieve what is required.

How realistic is this?

Each has unique interests. While some struggle in the understanding of concepts, others are ready to move on in a moment. Undeniably, the pace in a classroom format by its configuration must be detrimental to all.

While scoring the papers of a freshman level biology state standards exam offered as the final exam for the course, my thoughts were moved with concern. The items were in two groups, several multiple-choice questions followed by six written response open ended questions.

Again, with increasing alarm and dismay my grading work was interrupted with reflection upon the several hours of preparation and review before the students encounter with the test. The more I thought about it, the more overwhelming became the frustration. Countless questions darted through my mind. With every question, other questions popped up. In only a short time, my mind had become flooded with all sorts of concerns. Most if not all of these questions were without definitive answers. As well, that had been trying. However, consolation emerged in recognizing that questions even without answers are the beginnings of all success stories.

Could it be that the perceived shortfalls in education would be just beyond those questions?

By the time of the final exam, the young people that I attempted to help over several months appeared emotionally and physically drained after certainly an intense academic year that required numerous energy draining homework assignments and coursework projects doled out by other teachers coupled with the demands of sports and social life matters.

The students seemed no longer happy to be in school. The once bright looking high intensity youngsters now were coming to class tired, "burned out." They looked as if sapped of emotion, besieged from the good intentions of the compelling effort in teaching in every classroom encounter. They had taken on the behavioral mannerisms of the more aged unflappable upper class students whose typical response to a request might be the resigned "whatever."

Over six days, in the review of course material in an attempt to get a group of freshman ready for the biology final exam, in this case, the state standards test, that is what had been observed.

One student that remarkably did earn a near perfect score proclaimed, “The test was easy. I studied.”

Certainly, she had studied. Upon examination, her study notes were complete. Every word in review that was written on the marker board had been recorded in her notebook. On the other hand, the collected notes of others indicated that some did not prepare nor study as they might have. Their notes told the story. For some the notes were shoddy and incomplete. Margins of the notepaper included doodles. Other students chose not to write any notes. For the most part, their pages were blank. The discovery was disappointing.

I wondered, “Was I remiss? Should I have walked up and down the aisles checking to see if notes were being taken, if mental lapses were occurring? What would that accomplish? Would it be out of their inspired intentions or out of my insistence that provoked the note taking actions that were insincere or disingenuous?”

They had been given notice to write notes. They should have been aware of the importance of this comprehensive standards test given as a final exam. Overall, did the students measure up to the standards?

The average score was sixty-nine per cent.

I thought, “How could I have done better? Is sixty-nine per cent an acceptable average for freshman responding to a supposedly difficult state standards biology test?”

I will never know. No comparative baseline data was made available that might suggest that these students with my effort had done well or poorly.

In addition, was the test certifiable? How could it be? What would be the specific reference point objectives was one concern? Was it scrutinized by statistical item analysis? What were the difficulty coefficients for each test item and for the test as a whole?

Was the test biased or skewed to favor various standards? Did the test have congruency flaws? Was the test riddled with interfering language usage or word selection defects? Was the test neutral so that the personality and methodology of the teacher coupled with the dynamics of the students would be accommodated in a way that all students would have at least a reasonable opportunity to answer each question correctly? Importantly, what was known about students abilities as well as other qualities such as stamina, anything?

Assuming that the test was "perfect" and assuming that the student performance was in a satisfactory range, could they have done better if they were not exhausted? Is it possible to configure school so that debilitating fatigue is not a problem? Is it sensible that some "authorities" are recommending extending the school day and even the school year? When during an academic year do students wear down? When does their effort become hampered? When do those who do not fit in with the schooling system mentally drop out? Could it be about Thanksgiving time? Could it be before or after Spring break? When and for which students?

Some by their nature may have a higher endurance coefficient.

Furthermore, imagine a classroom filled with students. Each seated on hard chairs in rows, straight or obliquely placed, or in circles for that matter. No relief except for the five minutes between classes, they have to "listen" hour upon hour even record notes. They may be required to fill out a worksheet or perform some reading assignment or writing task albeit senseless in the minds of at least a few. The everyday ho-hum definitely can lead to the mental detachment that conjures up a perhaps justifiable "oh well" attitude.

Is it during these doldrums that listening set aside becomes gradually eroded into a serious shortcoming?

A congressman likely during a filibuster once said to his colleagues, "The mind can absorb only as much as the seat can stand."

Does that apply to the conventional classroom environment? Is what is applicable in congress equally applicable in school?

Realistically, if the intensity level is not at peak, a student may miss an important, critical, essential point that makes impossible the learning of tomorrow.

Hopefully that student would interrupt and inquire but how would the student know? Is it then that boredom intensifies and doodling begins?

Even if the student did know that some element had been missed, in general, would the self-conscious student ask the needed questions?

Should a teacher presume to know that students may be lost especially when the teacher feels comfortable with what can only be perceived? Will review provoke disengagement in others?

Should the teacher appeal for a review, the class response might be silence.

Now, what? What if students conceal their insights? How is that to be known? Can the teacher be accountable for that?

Only those initially courageous students might interrupt. It does not take too many experiences for students to become discouraged and untrusting realizing that any inquiry may be put aside with a leading phrase such as, "Had you paid attention, you would know the answer to what you are asking about."

Students do hear that nagging frequently enough, I am sure.

As a consequence of perhaps too many similar situations in too many environments, students lose heart and just accept the circumstances of school. They learn to stay in line with their peers. Their minds and hearts may respond, "Does it matter?" And, if you as a conscientious teacher do not get the desired student response that would enable maximum learning, might frustration set in? As a teacher, do you go on?

A polite though marginally motivated student who was typically withdrawn from classroom activities, remarked upon being queried, "I didn't learn anything in math today because I couldn't follow the material yesterday, the day before that, and the day before that. We just go on one page after another."

He agreed that his sense of dejection, his loss of heart, was being carried-over to other classes including my biology class.

I responded, "Indeed, that is regrettable. What would you have me do?"

He smiled saying, "I don't know."

I believed that he was sincere. He did not know.

When a student and more than likely many students out of hopelessness or weariness will not or cannot participate or would prefer to talk rather than study, instinctively the time space invariably gets filled with "teacher talk" because surely that is always construed as at least productive. That appears to be a conditioned teacher response. The alternative is to hand out worksheets that will keep the students busy even distracted.

Is teacher talk or student busy work what is desirable rather than an interaction that would achieve engagement leading to learning? What is the underlying impact of preconditioning that affects learning at any moment?

In effect, productivity may be minimal. That initiative to present more material might even be more devastating to morale. Teachers may be conveying to students something that has no foundation because they did not grasp the concept as aptly put, "from the day before and the day before that." And, if this is not enough, homework will finish them off.

How unfortunate is that? How can students on their own correctly apply what is not within their grasp?

The pseudo-justification for that is, "Whatever was not completed in class needs to be completed somewhere at some time."

So, yes! Homework is required but what kind of homework to accomplish what?

The appeal ought to be for mercy.

It can never be presumed that students are learning because they may present themselves even as pleasant and accommodating. A wholesome and even engaging disposition may be a mask covering mental withdrawal.

Learning cannot be taken for granted. Yet, a teacher needs to know if progress is being made.

However, will teacher persistence without student desire drive both farther off? What does it take to maintain a high level of success based teacher enthusiasm while positively gathering students into the learning process? Would a new or different approach make a difference? If so, what might that be?

4

Homework, a significant component in student life, is likely more encumbering than it is enriching.

Years ago, at the completion of her elementary school day, I met one of my daughters, Shellie. She was in the second grade and certainly did not weigh more than fifty pounds. As she emerged from the building, I immediately noticed that she was dragging her backpack over the sidewalk making her way to where I had parked. The sight of this struggle was too much for me to watch.

Quickly, I got out of the car, hurried to her to pick up the heavy load, and asked, "Why are you bringing all of this home?"

Shellie replied, "It's homework, Dad."

Puzzled, I said, "Well, didn't you have enough time to do your work in school? Were you goofing around?"

"No." she answered appearing alarmed. "This is what's leftover."

From there, holding her hand and carrying the backpack, we walked into the administrative office where I asked to meet with the principal, a dedicated topnotch professional with whom I had previously worked as a member on a committee concerned with classroom instruction, teaching and learning.

Now, with a smile and an exaggerated while lighthearted groan landing the much too heavy backpack on the principal's desk I asked, "Mrs. Jay, when is enough absolutely enough? Please, can you explain to me why my daughter has so much homework, homework in every subject that she must struggle truly dragging her books along?"

Of course, Mrs. Jay displayed astonishment and remarked, "I'll have to look into that."

Her comment to look into the matter was accepted as reasonable and sincere but I had to continue with my thoughts.

I said, "I appreciate all that you will do but what is this teacher thinking? She needs to understand that my daughter has a life at home. If this child goes to school all day and then works on homework through at least half of the evening, when does she have time to play and grow? When do we as a family get to know each other?"

Nothing had changed for Shellie. The homework continued maybe not quite as much.

However, I had become soured by homework for everyone at all levels unless it can be unquestionably justified. The debate does go on but consider the notion that homework should be outlawed.

What about that?

Oh of course, some might say, "If classroom time is used for student work that could be done at home, the teacher will have more time to cover the subject matter?"

That appears to have some merit and ought to be considered.

Given that, "What should a course of study include?"

Take into account that the school day is long enough and difficult enough with all of its encumbrances, should K-12 students have the after school time for enjoyment, some daily basic rest and relaxation or possibly working at a job?

Those students who labor on with their coursework are noticeably tired and even exhausted. The stress of add on homework can be overwhelming. Furthermore, with lengthy after school assignments, students may experience sleep deficiency. Supported with research, sleep is an essential requirement for the mental processing that properly seats learning.

Over time, confined by assorted assignments saturated with various requirements, students become as most understand, "burned out."

Unfortunately, some at the expense of their grades just refuse to do homework. Is putting someone at odds desirable at all?

Others blatantly share the work. Is to copy an assignment what was intended?

In general school rules prohibit this behavior but the hassle with students is not worth the contest that results.

Student to teacher, "I did not copy."

Teacher reply, "Yes, your paper is exactly like Robin's."

Student answer, "Well, it's a coincidence."

The dialog goes on back and forth. No one wins.

Of greater concern and most disconcerting should be that homework assignments are frequently included among the factors that determine grades. Student work sharing will compromise integrity and place a shadow of questionable authenticity upon grades. Subsequently, who will be able to describe or know the true academic worth of a student?

One day en route to the copy machine before classes were called to order, I had passed two students sitting on the hallway floor.

One said, "Did you finish your homework?"

The other responded, "Yeah, but it's not right. I just wrote down some numbers."

The first student replied, "It was hard. I wonder if anybody got any of them right."

The obvious student goal was get the homework done right or wrong. That is all that mattered. Then as the teacher would go over the homework in class, the students while copying the answers might mumble, "Oh. Why didn't you show this to me yesterday?"

However, note that this copying is teacher directed. It may well be viewed as acceptable even an excellent teaching method.

Some students may say, "Now I get it."

From the struggle with homework, what learning occurred, any? Could the teaching process have been structured differently? Maybe the homework assignment could have been up front handled in class with a comparable interactive dialog. Might that approach be better than prefaced with anxiety loaded homework?

Meaningfully working with another individual as two or perhaps several seriously think through the problems in the presence of a teacher is to be applauded. True learning may result along with the development of ancillary social and marketplace by-products fundamentally teamwork in a collaborative spirit. Real interaction leads to positive outcomes. This requires a prerequisite positive student mindset coupled with relaxed supervision. It is win/win. But, it is not commonplace.

Not to be too rigid over the notion of homework, two forms are acceptable. That is if the assignments maybe either a reading that can be understood and accomplished by the student or if on the other hand a creative writing task that can express a personal perspective. Reading a book as a homework assignment or writing an essay, story, or poem are reasonable because in all likeliness, these are something that do not require a correct answer and they are not limited by a class period time constraint. They represent involvement that may lead to the growth of imagination and the development of creativity.

The moments remain vivid when some interpretation of a literary composition was required. Failure was inevitable because published notes were still not widely available.

Who would know for sure what the author had intended years ago when the piece had been written?

Of course, the teacher always seemed to know precisely what the author had in mind. I had been there as a student. Nothing is more disconcerting than to have read a segment of literature only to discover during the next morning that your interpretation was "wrong," again!

Often I wondered, "How can that be? Is my opinion not worthy?

How is it that the teacher always knew? Was the exegesis something handed down by some insider passageway or by chance did the teacher know because of some never to be disclosed teacher privileged reference tucked away in a secure place or because of some direct communication with the dead?

Certainly, the anguish and suffering that I endured was more than anyone should have had to bear. Often the experience was humiliating and spirit breaking. That could be the underlying reason for preferring the virtues of science.

Would it not be better to go over the reading in class with explanations as you go?

In a fashion something like this, the teacher says to the students, "This is what the author appears to have meant. Generally, all scholarly explications do agree. What do you think, believe, or feel about that?"

The students would then be able to reply with a sense of confidence rather than hesitancy.

Would it not be better to guide and aid young minds in their responses to written words so that they might be able to develop the special insights?

A lot of coursework usually assigned for outside of class or library study requiring independent discovery of correct responses as may be necessitated in problem solving is better done in the classroom with the supervision and assistance of a teacher.

Burrhus F. Skinner and Sidney L. Pressey, during their day, took the position that being given a correct answer results in the positive reinforcement of learning. Both contributed to educational research in the programmed presentation of instruction with Skinner developing the methodology that can be described as linear while Pressey was involved in designing a branched style including a teaching machine for the delivery of instruction.

The corroboration is essential and critical. It precludes all attempts of the frequently played "cat and mouse" games in the classroom whereby the teacher suggests or implies, "I know the answer. See if you can figure it out or guess what it is."

Truly, I disliked teachers of that sort. Their self-righteousness was for me annoying and prohibitive. Work that might have been enjoyable was done out of necessity to achieve a higher order good, my goal.

The play-games-with-the-correct-answer approach to teaching and learning always seemed to be a turn-off on interest and motivation unlike the unraveling of a real maybe mind-boggling mystery.

That Skinner and Pressey are from a bygone era does not diminish the value of their work and findings. Unfortunately, like so many of the solid discoveries on teaching and learning, it has been set aside, forgotten, without regard for its inherent worth. Certainly, under some other name, the merit of their insights may be rediscovered eventually.

For sure, as I made my way through high school, I tried to get all of any homework completed before the end of the day. My after school job required having "free" time in the evenings. If I encountered difficulties I would take time immediately after school to seek out teachers as needed.

Math was one of my favorite subjects so I was always willing to do the work and tried to do it well. Vividly I recall some upsetting moments trying to figure out the problems of quite a few assignments especially at the college level.

The daily math routine then as it is similar if not the same for today went something like this. At the beginning of class, the assigned homework problems were written on the board. Students to do this were summoned or volunteered. With their effort now on display, the teacher would go over each problem correcting as needed and summarizing the solution while those present frantically copied as they observed. Some would sit looking on while likely pretending all the while that beforehand they knew all of the solutions.

Completing the review, the material for the next day, contingent upon the work of the day before, would be explained. With a few minutes left in the class period, the assignment would be given for example, "Solve the odd numbered problems, 1 through 27."

As the class period would wind down, the task at hand would be to work through as many problems as possible. The first two or three of those assigned were easy enough. But, in the evening, while alone at home or in the library, problem #5 would be difficult but not too difficult. After a few minutes of searching through the text the solution would become evident. Problem #7 would be more difficult but with a combination of effort and search, a sigh would erupt, a good feeling indicator, as the solution would be written out with answer circled. Now, problem #9 would be impossible and developing the correct answer for every problem thereafter always appeared progressively out of range more and more complex with a spin or twist that was not obvious even with thoughtful effort.

Compelled by some inner force to finish the assignment, the inevitable feelings of anguish gradually would set in. Not willing to give in clinging to fragments of hope, the search among a few hand-me-down books for examples that might provide a clue leading to a solution would begin. The effort was both exasperating and tiring, often futile.

Bewilderment coupled with the realization of uncompromising desperation would intensify along with the urge to throw the book across the room. The little mental voice would scream, "# @!"

In this situation, crying would not help. Thoughts would come and go. Ah, call a friend. Why bother? Each of us would be reinforcing the same anxiety adding to an already "bad" disposition. Your teacher is clear across town. It is late in the evening. Even if you could call for help, that would be unacceptable.

It does not get better with age. For the two calculus courses I needed in anticipation of graduate school, homework had been assigned at the end of each class meeting. Just as I had experienced in high school, I realized again. The first few problems of every take home assignment were easy enough but after that their solutions were beyond my capability.

In a spare back room in my house, I labored over those assignments. It was "practice" in problem solving that did not contribute to the grade. Nonetheless, it was work that needed to be mastered.

The room was furnished only with a desk, chair, and lamp. All over the floor of the room helter-skelter at times were calculus books and manuals. When in need of help to solve the specified problems I would crawl and scamper from book to book looking for anything that gave a clue that matched up with those problems of the assignment. Literally, as if in prayer, I scrambled on my knees. After sometimes what seemed to be hours of hunt and search, I would find an example that would lead to the coveted solution for most if not all of the problems. Eventually, I succeeded but only as a result of relentless determination. I wholeheartedly accepted the words of Winston Churchill: "Never give up. Never, never, never!"

Why do some young people give up on school believing that it is not within their reach?

In all likelihood they have felt helpless too and possibly too often. Recall the words spoken by a student already discouraged with school, "I didn't learn anything today because I didn't learn anything yesterday, because I didn't learn anything the day before that and the day before that."

Frequently enough, the homework assignment for elementary and middle school students and sometimes even for high school students imposes an additional and unnecessary responsibility upon parents who may well need moments of rest and relaxation for their own next day at work.

Who needs the aggravation?

Now, the daughter who at one time was dragging over the sidewalk her backpack with homework obligations is pondering over homework with both of her children, daughter and son.

Laughing she says, "Isn't it funny that I have to do what you did? I am now actually learning what I was supposed to have learned when I was their age."

It is good that my daughter can find some humor in the midst of the tears of her children pleading, "Mom, I gotta get this done by tomorrow."

Fortunately, their daily homework dose seems to be kept in moderation. Or, maybe the children are catching on to the driving forces of the system, frantically at work in school desperately trying to leave completed requirements in their desk, cabinet, or locker.

Ultimately, the notion that homework piled on keeps youngsters out of mischief cannot be substantiated. That is nonsense, a point of view without merit. The argument cannot be supported. Most likely, those individuals that do the homework are not the ones who would engage in mischief or get into trouble anyway.

Maybe, in the zealousness to accomplish as much as possible, homework giving teachers overlook judiciousness.

Should homework givers be held accountable for their indiscretion or praised for doing their job as expected at least by some? What are the essential demands of a course or even school? Is homework absolutely necessary? What has to be accomplished in school for students to become marketplace-ready Good Citizens of Earth?

Is it likely that students do enough work in school? Should they be asked to take work home? Are those who assign additional coursework not asking students to work overtime? Is homework a reasonable expectation and demand? What can be the justification for homework?

What if a student while doing their homework assignment has a problem or needs to ask a question about the work at hand? To whom does the student turn for help? Should parents become obligated and though even on a good day might not be able to help?

True, homework hotlines have become available but should the teacher not provide the help for the work that was assigned? Should the assigning teacher be at the end of the hotline?

That would change the outcome for many.

Of course, the issue is controversial. However, the most important factor in this decision is whether or not any given amount of homework correlates positively with overall improved test scores or real learning. Clearly, the answer is a resounding, "No!" Again, the "Law of Unexpected Consequences" applies. As the amount of homework requiring more than one hour per day increases, overall student performance tends to decreases.

Certainly, as the amount of homework is increased, the time

needed for exploration will be diminished and likely the amount of nagging will be proportionately increased, "Did you do your homework? Well, go to your room and finish it!"

Furthermore, would after school free time benefit students by giving them the opportunity to "bond" with other family members as well as giving them the time for recuperation before the start of the next day of work? So, what is enough? Should the homework be piled on top of an already packed school day? Has school become more demanding than the workplace of the parents?

5

The biology grade of a wonderful young man had slipped from an A minus to a B plus. This elicited an inquiry from Mom, "What has happened with my son's grade?"

I asked the mother if she were employed.

"Yes," she replied.

Inquiring further, "And, how many hours do you work each week?"

After a moment of thought, she responded, "Maybe forty-five hours on average."

I said, "Well, let's see how many hours Jimmy puts into school. First, he is in school seven and one half hours each day; then each day in addition he has perhaps two hours of homework, plus four hours of weight training and football practice. Now, that adds up to thirteen and one half hours each day or sixty-seven and one half hours per week not including the five hours or so for the weekly football game. For at least one semester during the football season, Jimmy actually works a lot more than you."

We smiled. She understood.

Consider the typical school day times five days a week. It has to be grueling. Except for a retreat, no one in business and industry would ever consider demanding as much from their employees, essentially sitting in meetings, attentive to every word, taking notes, and interacting with a positive disposition throughout the day every day. Yet, this sort of demand is placed upon every student day in and day out.

As these demands would be ludicrous in the marketplace, they certainly would be equally destructive to morale.

And, consider this. Students have to ask to use the "potty room" at the risk of being denied. Of course, the justifications may be, "It's likely a ploy. They'll get into mischief. We don't want them wandering in the halls."

Certainly, the rationale and many others may seem to be reasonable.

However, it is possible that the anticipated wayward behavior of some students contains a message.

Now, as standards are imposed, as schools are expected to do more, the inclination is to expect more time on task, to add on and on to the school day as well as the school year.

Is that reasonable? Is it reasonable for students to begin school before the Sun comes up? Why is it expected?

As has been reported, a positive correlation exists between increased learning and giving students in even the upper grades more play time.

Remarkable! Again, the "Law of Unexpected Consequences" may apply getting results contradictory to what might be anticipated. More studies may be needed not for the students but for the educators to confirm or debunk the report.

As Jimmy was, are other students by well intending but thoughtless parents expected to overwork? What about the homework for Jimmy? How much does he really need, twenty minutes a night for each course for every school day, ten hours of "overtime" each week? Except for those salaried and higher up on the administrative ladder, who would be expected to put in that amount of "extra" work for their company?

Most of all, when is it then that children have a chance to be children? When will the foundations be established that will support worthy, noble, and Good Citizens of Earth?

As I had observed years ago during a family Thanksgiving celebration, a father scolded his one year old son for getting tangled in the antenna and electrical wires leading to the television set. Overhearing this, the grandfather chided in response, "If you expect your little boy to behave as a man today, when will he be a little boy?"

Over the long run, what impact might such well intended admonishments on children have on their mental development? Will it stifle curiosity? And, why worry about inquisitiveness?

Likely, this attribute is a foremost quality that needs to be preserved. Everyone needs to be asking "why." It is the crucial word leading to answers and problem solving.

Unless secure with an inquiring mind, why search for meaning, why investigate, explore, probe, or scrutinize? Why act? Why do anything at all?

What needs to be realized is that school of its very nature is an arduous and exhausting place where more is told than can be comprehended and retained where the best efforts to sustain and culture interest fall short. For many if not most of those attending, it is not at all satisfying, not at all like "fun."

Then, when are little girls and boys children and when are teenagers given the needed prerogatives to grow into adults finding their way? When and how does a maturing individual develop the skills of an adult?

In the school regime and through its prescriptions, curiosity is not typically tolerated and consequently, does not thrive. The outcome is that disenchantment will be enhanced. Later in life, as employees, the many "short changed" individuals may be admonished for not "thinking out of the box."

What should be done to solve the conundrum?

Considering many secondary school students as I recently have encountered the matter of greatest concern is will these individuals do the day-to-day classroom work?

Some apparently are bogged down for countless reasons other than those imposed by school. Some students are tired because of the outside of school demands that they deal with most nobly a job flipping burgers or perhaps babysitting. These tend to sleep with eyes opened or closed even though sleeping in class is prohibited. But, what option is left for them?

Some teenagers have babies of their own. They want to be with their children especially when a child is sick. These young parents are not thinking about schoolwork. One student was anxious to get a driver's license so that without having to ask his parents for a ride he could visit his child several miles away. What are his in school thoughts?

Many are distracted by family problems that result from parents who have abandoned them or have been incarcerated for serious offenses. Others have to deal with the constraints of having committed crimes themselves. What might be their major focus?

A number of students have issues that result from a divorce. These may be polite but quietly rebel by choosing not to do any of the assigned work. By failing, they appear to want to hurt one or both of their parents, even their well intending teachers. Their actions seem to be shouting, "I'll show you. What do you think of that?"

Countless students are just poorly nurtured. Socially and interactively they do not cope well. The childhood and the adolescence of these students perhaps had been mismanaged either by parents, guardians, or custodians. These tend to talk and ignore any effort in teaching. They demand attention. Worse, they distract others from doing as well as they could do. How does that get remedied?

Of course, the school system does have student management mechanisms in place to deal with some of these derived unacceptable classroom behaviors. Nonetheless, poor behavior by any student is prohibitive and limits overall productivity.

How can these students be engaged in schoolwork when their life's problems are for them greater than the possibility of future payoffs from good grades or any achievement ideal that can be proposed?

The system requires that the scores of these various individuals will be averaged among the scores of all the others that go into comparative studies and measurements of teacher and school successfulness.

Then, some students earn out of some justification an Individual Education Plan. These excusable students have garnered the benefit of someone who at least tacitly supports stated ambitions. While some claims may be legitimate, many of these plans are in effect a license for laziness and needless demanding behaviors that thereby shift the responsibility for learning to the teacher and limit others.

The following is an example of one student among maybe many presumably worthy students similarly supported with an IEP. The student will be:

- Provided with photocopies of the teacher's notes or the notes of another student;
- Provided with auditory, visual, or kinesthetic modes of presentation;
- Given cues regularly by asking questions providing for think time;
- Excused from reading orally in class to avoid embarrassment;
- Monitored for possible frustration;

- Encouraged to ask for assistance;
- Given an assignment sheet, notebook, or monthly calendar; and
- Given extra time for the completion of tests.

This privileged student must now be set apart from all of the other students given every feasible accommodation without any requirement for initiative. Should some classroom difficulty arise, this student has someone to blame. What a deal!

Yet, regardless of every afforded consideration, every call for participation, this student persisted in sleeping. He was not without learning means because on a few occasions, perhaps on the occasional "rare day," this individual performed as well as the best students in the class. Disregarding positive feedback, this student would repeatedly go back to "business as usual" in the classroom. He seemed to work only to fail. When given an assignment or a test, often he would hand in a blank sheet. What was the message?

No doubt some really good teacher might be able to explain what should have been done to lift the performance of this wayward individual in a class of twenty-two all of which needed support. It was beyond me.

The routine for performance enhancement might be, "You could have . . . maybe if . . . well, please try."

In the meantime, while placating the requirement for attention, what is to be expected of the other, twenty-two in this case or even twenty-seven students? Should they remain patient while their time for learning is set aside? Why?

During one conversation, this IEP protected student revealed that he did not like the school he was in. He was in fact angry because of it.

After a divorce, the young man was granted the right to reside with his father who did not live in the school district of preference. Subsequently, he was transferred to save the out-of-district tuition fees his father otherwise would have had to pay. Odd as it may be or is it odd that at his previous school the young man did not have the advantage of an IEP.

During an after-the-school year luncheon, the day after the last day of classes commonly riddled with pranks and an array of student outbursts, the principal remarked, "Yesterday was truly difficult for us but that is why they need us."

Can anything be done to improve upon the lackluster performance of many of the students not so much because in academic areas they lag behind and not so much because they need us to generally help them along but most of all because truly we need them?

Are teachers and schools too rigid or not rigid enough in imposing demands? What methods should be used to get into the hearts and minds of those whose problems at least for them are far greater than can be imagined, are seen as devastating, are in fact prohibitive?

Are options available that will get youngsters to where they need to be ideally equipped for the marketplace and beyond without exhausting them? Are methods of teaching available that will help students to learn within their range of constraints while not tiring them excessively so that they become even more discouraged or despondent?

Obviously, many more questions about education can be asked and among those quite a few are likely beyond a simple answer.

6

While nearing the completion of work leading to a Bachelor of Science degree in Liberal Arts with a major in Biology and a cognate in Philosophy anticipating graduate school, a former employer, the owner of an art studio, encouraged me to enter the teaching profession. A biology teacher was needed for a recently established high school. I was not trained to be a teacher. I had never taken a course in education.

I thought, "Why not? I could do this."

I began teaching high school students as I knew how, as I had been taught, not unlike how maybe farmers farm as more or less aptly described by an educator I met along the way. My only available reference was to selectively do what was done to me. During the first days on the job as a beginning teacher my interest increased daily. I became intrigued by the processes that could make my effort efficient and effective so that students could become more resourceful and successful. Quickly, though without foundation, I had begun to think in terms of "do this to get that." I enjoyed the work. The challenges became inspiring. I was enthusiastic about all aspects, preparing, presenting, and following up.

Working with young and happy people who were excited, creative, and curious a lot of wonderful and worthwhile field trips as well as get-together sing and dance in-school events came about. I still have memorabilia, the posters that the students had made and photos of them enjoying the moments that were shared.

After teaching for only a short time, I realized that everything about a teacher as a person is on the line always under the keen scrutiny of a teenager every moment while in front of a class or working directly offering one-on-one or small group assistance.

Today, I realize that the school oriented teenagers that I had been teaching, none had given up on learning, were truly alert to what had been going on and quite honestly judgmental about it. Had I been doing poorly, they would have been the first to speak up. Unfortunately, they offered no verbal feedback and I was not experienced enough to read student body language or to listen to what they were saying in silence.

Be that as it may, since I was new in teaching, each day I did look for some feedback. I felt good about what I was doing but I continued to wonder, "Do they feel as I do?"

In a moment of insecurity, perhaps anxiety, I approached the principal. For what it is worth, he said, "Presume that your work is at least satisfactory until you hear otherwise from me."

I was surprised and disappointed with the answer. But, over the years, I have come to realize that is about all that could be expected.

In a little over one year I had completed work for teacher licensure and certification and remarkably, over the next three years, I had qualified for several National Science Foundation summer long science education programs. Timing could not have been better. I was developing insights, skills, and know-how. I was on the cutting edge of newly developed programs in biology education. I was in graduate school. It was great.

My first stunning lesson came during my second teaching year. The presentation on electricity to an eleventh grade physical science class was a disaster. I thought my effort was as good as it gets but unaware that the students were not catching on even from the onset I continued on and on mentally basking in unfounded delight. The students did not have a clue. They did not understand a word of what was intended. Their polite behavior was misleading. Then unknown to me, the telltale sign in the classroom was a deafening quiet.

Fortunately, after the misdirected teaching episode, Betsy, a courageous young lady stayed on for a moment and said to me, "You talked about this for an hour when will you explain it?"

The explanation took a week.

Overall, I was the one who had learned, indeed an excruciating lesson. It was, "Do not overestimate the effectiveness of your effort. Because a concept is clear in your mind does not guarantee necessarily that as it may be presented, it will be equally clear in the minds of the students. Clarity in your mind is not good enough. Clarity in the mind of students is all that matters. Only if what is presented is understood and results in learning is your effort good enough."

In the classroom of today as I have found it, while more may be desired and while students may be encouraged to interrupt and ask for explication or provide feedback, they tend to "duck and hide." They are not willing to expose themselves, ask for explanations or remark, "I don't get it." Likely, it is a peer pressure thing that demands this kind of reservation. Necessarily, teenagers do not want to stand out in what may turn out to be an embarrassing situation and they are unwilling to take a chance even if their effort is remarkable.

How and when did they learn this general "lay low" tactic? Is this behavior the outcome of conditioning developed in previous environments coupled with possible fear of stepping out of the presumed boundaries of the teenage culture? Was it learned in their early years? Were they reprimanded or chastised too much from early on in school? Did their friends harass them for their outspokenness? Is it a "primal brain" thing?

Once I said to a friend, "While you are okay, I don't like your behavior."

That comment had led to a significant realization, the great difference between a person and what they do. What individuals do is a consequence of how they have been treated. They might be able to control that with determination but who they are is more than how they act or how they conduct themselves. Who they are is sacred and deserves reverence. How they perform may or may not earn respect. How they treat others may deserve tolerance.

We do need those we teach especially those in high schools. We do need to be up-front in what is taking place in a setting of respect for their effort and in general reverence for their inherent worth.

In five years after signing on as a teacher, I had completed work for Master of Arts and Doctorate in Education degrees with majors in Biology, Chemistry, and Teacher Education.

Along the way, in working on my research, I had been introduced to individualized instruction and subsequently stumbled onto strategic analysis management systems commonly employed in business and industry. It made sense to consciously apply these techniques in teaching. Every conceivable detail in the instructional process could be isolated, defined, and evaluated for its specific contribution to learning. Taking advantage of both method and approach, I had been able to design guided discovery teaching strategies that were efficient and effective, for me the ultimate goal.

Thoroughly convinced, regardless of level, schools should be accommodating to this approach as it engages students more directly in the learning processes.

With hope, some recently imposed accrediting requirements may be accidentally forcing this outcome, the improvement of teaching in the framework of a system linked to basic analytical processes. However, teachers will have to incorporate their own guided discovery methods within the context of the already selected and publisher influenced constraining materials that are fixed and in place in conjunction with state imposed standards that as may be realized are generally flawed and may in reality be working against desirable innovation. Actually, to get it right in education, it ought to be the other way around.

Again, dare anyone take a chance? Who will speak up? Who will stand out?

With the application of these guided discovery methods and systems analysis processes, anticipated student achievement outcomes were significantly better than had been expected. Teaching for me became more absolute. Students learned more in less time. The groundwork for substantive teacher accountability was in place.

For the next sixteen years, I had served as the science department chairperson for a small college. While in that capacity, the department nearly quadrupled in its enrollment. This was due mainly to a comprehensive student hands-on workshop program that I had put together working with area teachers and students on the development of science project skills and procedures. The program was coupled with science paper contests and highlighted with annual banquets for the recognition of student excellence in science.

In addition, I had earned a rather substantial National Science Foundation grant for the implementation and study of individualized instruction systems for Introduction to Biology, General Biology, Anatomy and Physiology, and Microbiology. These instructional design systems were then as they are now, directly applicable to the development of distance learning and home school programs.

By the conclusion of the grant, I realized that I had to turn my sights to other opportunities. At that time, Terrel Bell, Secretary of Education, had published the report, *A Nation at Risk: The Imperative for Educational Reform*, an appraisal on the status of education in the United States compared with the rest of the advanced countries. I had begun adjusting my teaching to accommodate the proposed marketplace needs teaching for purposefulness and application. Along these lines, I had begun presenting training and development programs for area businesses.

It was not long before "the offer that cannot be refused" came along. Given the job of Materials/Operations Manager, I left education looking forward to learn what business and industry really needed anticipating that at some time in the future, I would be able to apply those insights in education.

After twelve years in industry and on the brink of retirement, the opportunity to again teach in a private school setting had come along.

I had always considered myself as a good teacher. Always my marks on student evaluations had been in the range of good to superior. The occasional unsolicited often handwritten remarks from students confirm the appraisals.

The comments made by the two daughters of the dean I had once worked under were especially satisfying. After completing four-year degrees, the dean conveyed to me that the older of the two had said to him that of all the college professors I had presented myself as the most knowledgeable in my subject area. Later, he confided that the younger daughter had mentioned to him that pedagogically, I had been her most skillful professor knowing just how to present material so that it was clear and understandable.

More recently, a student wrote on his final exam, "Your class was the most informative class I've had. You made us think about things we've never thought about. Thank you."

Another wrote, "If the goal of all teachers is to impact student's lives – you have achieved it."

Many of those "in jeopardy" students that I would encounter frequently inquired, "Are you coming back next year?"

My response would be, "Should I?"

To my reply, these students consistently would answer, "Yes."

Interested, I would say, "Why?"

A typical comment would be, "Because you are a good teacher."

When I would query, "What makes you think so?" they would invariably say, "Because you care."

It was difficult for them to explain how they knew that I cared. Just the same, they persisted, "But, you do care."

When I accepted each and every teaching position, I insisted that my sole purpose was to help students learn. Indeed, more recently that had been a greater challenge than anticipated. My return to the classroom would be perplexing for me. At times it would be agonizing and I would often become filled with dismay and disillusionment, more than could have been imagined.

Daily, I would wonder, "What happened to the educational environment I once knew and enjoyed so much?"

When asked for my thoughts, typically I would say, "Teaching today is the most difficult job that I have ever had."

The student quest for right answers as if the answers to questions were the end-all, the ultimate achievement in learning, had been upsetting. This student appetite would be in reality contrary to the very heart of teaching, at least to the substance of teaching that mattered to me. It would be incongruous with the development of concepts that would lead to problem solving founded upon the integration of ideas, ideas that might lead to new discoveries that just might advance the frontier of knowledge.

Equipped with answers, the students that I would meet presumed that they adequately and responsibly fulfilled their obligation in learning.

"Why?" I asked myself. "Does anybody know how this absurd way of thinking got started?"

Regardless, the student mindset seemed to be, "If you can get the right answers, all will be fine, all is good, you've done your job."

The derived gratification for their accepted accomplishment was without question, "Now, will you leave me alone to do as I please?"

Why the intense focus upon and the overwhelming contentment with answers? Instead, why not seek understandings? Or, why not go for analysis, synthesis, or evaluation even critical thinking and problem solving?

As I continued to search to understand, I continued in asking, "What about a new approach? Will all be 'better' if the students were to get it straight, if the students were to seek comprehension, to tease apart information, to compile as well as possibly assemble data into new configurations?"

Arguably, emphasis needs to be shifted to the meaningful use of knowledge in higher order cognition and in problem resolution. At least from what I experienced in industry, it seems to be the right alternative.

Is answer seeking something unique about the students of today? Is it okay? Have students become accustomed to some distorted use of answer driven objectives, goals that are forthcoming from standards that are intended to guarantee "no child will be left behind" early on or later in school and in life?

Could the student fixation upon answers alone result from the noble well intended application of classroom methodology of work sheets and copying of teacher made notes coupled with overbearing parental pressure that appears to be linked to the unfortunate aspiration derived notions that good grades are the cornerstone structures leading to "college of choice" entry? Or, is it the exit strategy leading to a diploma and some kind of job? Is it a way of self-protection and self-preservation?

Apparently, an undermining notion has emerged, that if students can be kept busy and fully occupied, then each school day will go by according to some groove as maybe a canyon is carved by a swiftly flowing river. The students will have been keen at their job, time on task can be quantified, seat time can be certified, and the teacher will leave the building without having faced a challenge. Apparent learning is going on. Is it?

I recall during my daily planning period at some time or another often passing by a classroom and noticing the day-in and day-out routine of a particular teacher. The room was dim, lighted only by the lamp of the overhead projector. The students were always feverishly copying notes from the in front of the room screen as the teacher standing next to the projector read to the class the exact same words as projected.

I wondered, "If these notes are so important, why not just copy and distribute them? What cost would it be to the school? With this procedure, what cost is it to the students? What are they learning anyway, copying?" And, how many exposures of this kind are really needed if how to copy is the goal?"

Certainly, as these students transcribe the notes, their minds are not locked into the message. More likely they are concentrating on getting the words onto their papers.

Could it be that earlier adjustments in teaching and evaluation methods coupled with the recently imposed requirements for academic excellence now expressed as a set of specific standards and correlated answer accommodating objectives are the stimuli or at least in part the contributors to this kind of classroom methodology?

These may appear to be plausible causes. Of course, others are possible.

Is any of it acceptable? Should teachers design instruction that will encourage the attainment of higher order uses of the standards, taken as absolutes?

In my classes, I did not use many textbook dependent worksheets. I worked with students by asking leading questions and by working to engage them in thinking. In anticipation of lab work, rather than hand out procedures, I asked the students to write up their own procedures after an introduction of what the lab would be about.

Furthermore, the textbook was not read chapter after chapter but was used as a reference whenever and however needed. Diagrams were studied and analyzed for what they represented. Often, students were asked to point with their fingers at what they should be seeing. At various times, I would walk the aisles checking with them to get feedback that they were indeed following along. I needed to see for myself. That was my assurance. If something were amiss, I wanted to fix it immediately. I took nothing for granted. Overall, students were expected to read and think about the reading and then think about the concept and then read again if necessary to expand their thoughts.

"Extra credit" was never permitted unless all of the prescribed creditable work had been completed. Then, it became unnecessary.

How can the students do extra if they have not done the essential work?

The substitution of work would be a distortion of the intended course. And, "outside work" was never assigned unless all of the "inside work" had been completed. Again, this would be a misleading alteration of the course. Lastly, homework was seldom if ever assigned. I preferred that all of the class work be done with me as the teacher available to assist as I could.

Sure, I would fall behind in the prescribed schedule but what good would be keeping up if the students without the foundation for learning were then truly left behind? I would not be able to justify that to them knowing that for some arbitrary structure, I would literally fail them in whatever might be their attempt in learning.

Eventually, I would change teaching assignments, going public. In this setting I would encounter in a single classroom of twenty-four accompanied by great contrasts in student ability and performance, several students who could not focus on schoolwork because their personal life issues were enormously complex; a disgruntled student in foster care for whom I was a M----- F----- (you know in street talk what the abbreviation stands for); and challenged students who struggled with learning who were so wonderful and deserving that I would constantly stress over all of the classroom distractions that kept me from assisting them as I would have liked. For me this incredible mix of students was prohibitive of the best that could be offered, an abomination. But that is the way it was as I had encountered an unacceptable assignment. Little if anything could be done if anything was done to change the situation for any of us except to cope relying upon the limited permissible tools.

Moving on, I accepted responsibility in teaching two sections of a multi-section course driven by power point presentations, the presumed "end all" of good teaching. All lectures of the over enrolled and under facilitated classes were to be conducted in this creatively stifling disheartening lockstep impersonal format of textbook copied graphics and captions. Through some kind of ingeniousness, in an attempt to accommodate every student need, the presentations were internet accessible. Any incentive to attend class had been set aside except for what students might derive from their laboratory experiences. Though student appraisals of my effort were exceptional, one negative out of fifty-three, my effort was above all under appreciated.

Hope should not be forsaken. I went on to a small college with a pleasant atmosphere supported with students keenly interested in learning in developing personal wholesomeness. The opportunity would be gratifying. Again, I would be able to help students learn.

7

Everyone in every enterprise one way or another is held accountable. For the quality of workmanship, each person appears to be answerable to someone. Why? Is it assumed, "There is no free lunch" whether it be wages or some other reward? But, is the principle equally supportable in education?

Understandably, the answer is not exactly.

In their workplace, teachers are not manufacturing parts or producing assorted tangibles. They are not placing metal sheets into a press that will form fenders or fitting components into some purposeful entity. Teachers work with potentially opposing forces, individuals who are resilient, who can shape their outcome by determined choices influenced as they may be. Consequently, what is a reasonable evaluation method for teacher workmanship?

While a community does have a vested interest in the outcomes of classroom effort and rightly should call out for accountability some variable measure of indulgence seems appropriate adjusted according to the nature of student responsiveness.

Adequately answering to the external demands is challenging because increasingly the latitudes of teachers have been stripped away. More and more, they have become classroom functionaries not the authors of the content, the quantity, and often the method. They have become further burdened with responsibilities well beyond teaching in a subject area.

Progressively, teachers have been relegated to occupy a space, to present information according to some prescribed structure or curriculum, and control the behavior of those assigned to them while working under restrictive conditions such as an Individual Education Plan for one or for several students simultaneously.

Then, how can it ever be known if a teacher is truly doing their job? Are the right questions being asked? What is the measuring stick by which they should be measured?

Perhaps the significant and conclusive qualities are not readily quantifiable.

At what level will the proverbial bar be placed? Across the board, will the definitive factors be applied consistently? Should teachers have a voice in the measurement of their performance?

Generally, even if thoughtful, their voice has been disregarded. Decisively, George Bernard Shaw wrote, "Those who can do. Those who can't teach."

I heard this all too often. It is offensive.

Suggested, teachers are shallow. Presumed, teachers are not trustworthy. Implied, teachers need to be watched. Conclusion, teachers are not professionals.

For those who take this point of view, consider that you are absolutely out of touch with the teaching enterprise. You are without question wrong in your thinking and certainly are ignorant at least concerning what the enterprise of teaching is about. On the contrary, teaching with all of its merits can be more fascinating and captivating than any endeavor other than possibly bringing peace to the world.

At one time in my teaching career, I heard a lot of unreasonable discrediting remarks. I have persisted in my philosophy predicated upon a cherished line from the Optimist Creed, "Give so much time to the improvement of yourself that you have no time to criticize others."

Often put aside, teachers are viewed as a necessary encumbrance to be tolerated, frequently challenged on their value and sometimes confronted on their personal alignments.

In support of this kind of disregard, at one place of employment, several years ago, near the end of a school day, the intercom screeched, "Ms. Bobbie, please report to the office immediately at the end of period."

Panic overcame the teacher because her father was a test pilot. She immediately thought something dreadful may have happened to him. At the sound of the bell, she hurriedly made her way down the stairway and nearly running negotiated the hallways flooded with wandering students.

When she arrived at the office out of breath, sternly she was greeted by one of the secretaries, "Do you know that you had collected two Canadian quarters with the social club money?"

Until this day, who would really care? But, it does say something about the way that teachers are sometimes perceived, regarded, and mistreated.

At this same school where stationery supplies were provided to faculty, a new pen from the stores and supplies would not be issued unless a secretary ascertained that its ink had been completely consumed. One would always check. Using the to be discarded pen the secretary would vigorously scribble across a piece of paper, if any ink showed up, it would generate a smile with the words more or less surly spoken, "It still works." The pen would be returned.

As others, I purchased my own pen. This was personally less expensive than the perk.

Worthy or not, at another school, as a cost saving measure, inspectors would visit classrooms to see that all LED (light emitting diode) lamps, even those on ground fault electrical outlets when not in use were "off." All in all, if the LEDs on this sort of appliance were never "off" the expense to the school would likely be pennies over a year. Regardless, it was the responsibility of the teacher to disarm each outlet. And, a printer or computer not shut down at the end of the day would earn more than a frown. Notices were sent to faculty who overlooked their responsibility. Certainly in that, more energy was consumed and more effort wasted than the cost of electricity that might otherwise have been incurred.

When confronted with this demand, I thought, “This too is senseless, bordering on ridiculous, too extreme, not deserving of serious consideration. Next, will teachers be asked to again whittle pencils?”

Arguably, while publicly saluted with an occasional tribute or showered with some verbal admiration, conceivably spurious and shallow recognitions, teachers are scrutinized and more often than not criticized for their performance. They may well be the scapegoats of the system.

Their limited influence in the affairs of education confirms this notion that teachers are not highly regarded. They are the “doers” rather than the planners and the executors of the matters of school. They are the ones without input into the system, the ones scrutinized under the watchful eye of the community, the ones when in the classroom who may be abused by the children of that same community. Still, they are held to validate their true worth. The burden of proof is upon them.

A visiting student from Kenya observing an insulting student said to me, “In my country, students are not like that. They treat teachers as their fathers.”

I replied, “As you can see, many as this student undoubtedly do the same in this country.”

Presuming that teachers do not know much about the requirements of the “outside world,” summer internship programs have been set up to help them along, to educate the supposed unaware isolated “book worms” in the ways and means, the “A, B, C’s” of business and industry. However, business and industry might be served at least as well by coming into the schools to understand the conditions that prevail, the circumstances that have been imposed by their actions upon teachers.

So, why is it that the community does not enter the school to find out how they can be supportive and assist in what is needed?

Any efforts along these lines can be perceived as token at best. Some schools during the first days of the academic year boast of such programs but afterwards the efforts seem to fade out of sight. Many of those thought to be interested in becoming involved apparently get caught up in their own business needs. So, the community remains unaware of the constraints that confine the world of teachers and limit the context established for schools.

Are teachers the knowledgeable ones of their profession? Would anyone go to a financial manager for an appendectomy? Then, why does a community go to a guy who sells swimming pool chemicals, makes seat covers, builds boats, fits eyeglasses, manufactures glue, or dabbles in politics for input on how teachers should get along in their profession and how schools should function?

Apparently, the answer is founded in ownership. A few and the likely outspoken within a community claim the responsibility. If they did not, who would?

As they have done in the past, communities have become accustomed to look to those eager representatives from business and industry even past principals with administrators and professors in the college and university circle as their guideposts, as "fix-it" directors.

However, if these considered advisors had hit the mark, all public school students would be competitive within the global marketplace.

Is that a worthy conclusion? Why not get input from teachers whose job it is to pass down the heritage, to educate?

Teachers have studied. They have learned. Even, they have

been certified and licensed by some standard of measure. The bottom line is obvious. It is with disregard that teachers are relegated to a place of no significance even within the realm of their profession.

In the span of my memory, no other profession has been so restricted. Could it be because teachers are without a more or less exclusive insider vocabulary that serves to relegate the outsider?

It makes sense that if legal advice were needed, an attorney wisely would be called. Then, when it comes to matters of school, similarly, teachers ought to be called. They should be asked to not only execute the course of study but also from the onset decide how it should progress and as important should settle on what it ought to contain.

The shortfall may be that teachers work collaboratively in committees and only slowly progress in accomplishment. Consequently, whatever the task may be, it has to be expedited for them by some outside source that presumably "knows how to get things done." However, patience is a virtue. Teachers do measure up. Their work is time limited. Regularly, they meet benchmark constraints.

For sure, with the leverage of community leadership, it has been easy to reposition the blame for any inadequacy that may be perceived within the schools. "Teachers you're it." Of course, one has to realize the consequence of pointing no matter how cleverly it is done.

Can this be justified? How does this kind of overbearing attentiveness get resolved so that teachers are truly enabled thereby permitting schools to become meaningful and facilitating so that students find learning worthwhile? Is it possible that communities tend to rely upon needless outside expertise for insights when in reality the diamonds overlooked are in their proverbial backyard?

Given their unique autonomy, charter schools appear to have

merit.

Overall, communities are inconsistent likely because as they are inclined, it is easier to judge than to understand because individuals generally walk only in their own shoes.

Representatives from business and industry though well intentioned do not have the insight to create the alignment that is needed. The teaching colleagues of higher education cannot provide the needed insight either because by some observers and students, they tend to be out of touch, perhaps driven by or preoccupied with the demands of the insidious rule, "publish or perish." Their students, some of them prospective teachers, may be well trained in the theoretical aspects of education but are lacking in some of the basic skills of teaching and the requirements for learning within their subject area.

However, given what is, presume that state imposed standards are acceptable as a measure for accountability. Now what?

Randomly, pick out a standard, any standard will do. Now, imagine that to properly teach to this standard, eight elements represented by delineating objectives need to be achieved. A qualification is in order. Each of these objectives represents some significant part of the standard. Only when together is the presumed concept of the standard complete.

Now, here comes the ultimate exam that will test the achievement of the students that reflects the accomplishment of the teacher. As I have experienced, only one selected question is used to represent the entire standard. This course might distort the outcome. Selecting only one of eight representative questions is justified to make the test a manageable length for the available classroom time. However, in so doing, this might be in effect an outright injustice for both student and teacher.

What can be concluded if several students answer the question incorrectly? Did the students fail because they did not care, because their baby was not feeling well, for some personal reason, or does it reflect a poor teaching effort? Could it be that neither is at fault? Could it be that the question was not answered correctly because of a wording incongruity? Can some opposite conclusions be drawn if several students answered the question correctly?

We need to go back to the scenario to the one question that is presented for each standard of a course of study, for example a total of forty-five for a course that I once had been assigned to teach. If this number appears inadequate for conclusions to be made either representing failure or success, then how many questions about the various elements of the standard should be asked before a proper conclusion can be drawn about student competency or mastery as well as teacher effectiveness?

Take this approach to the eventual point of dilemma. Forty-five standards have been written. Each would require teaching and learning between seven and fifteen aspects, elements, or objectives, twelve on average. If questions were written to cover every element of every standard, the test would be composed of possibly 540 questions. This may be considered far too many criteria for students to deal with during a one hour class period. Obviously, the number of test items would have to be reduced.

The vexing problem is to determine exactly or even more or less how many questions would be reasonable.

Would a reasonable test include one hundred, two hundred, or more items? How many would be needed? Does anybody know?

If one hundred questions were provided, this would represent only 18.5 per cent of the academic course. How comfortable would one be deriving conclusions based on the representative data? Of course, how comfortable would one be making financial investments with a scant twenty per cent of the available information?

The potentials of this projection can become wearisome, indeed, a conundrum. The possibilities are virtually endless but the potential picture should be sufficient to grasp the problem.

When employed in industry by an engine parts manufacturer, my job required the management of materials and operations processing. The company made after-market engine components and some original equipment pistons for air compressors. In addition to a variety of responsibilities, I ordered raw materials, posted manufacturing schedules, worked directly with customers, and ordered the shipment of finished goods. Accomplishment at the end the day could be measured by the quantity of quality parts that had been packaged and loaded for delivery on a truck waiting at the dock.

In teaching, I miss the sense of achievement at the end of the day. Those students that I have worked with most recently fall short, at least in my estimation. My results are not impressive. Frequently, during my drive home after school, I would think, "A lot of effort went into the work of the day but the imaginary truck at the school shipping dock was empty without any of the important commodity, student learning."

People are inclined to tell me, "Oh, don't be hard on yourself. You have impacted some in your class. You just don't know it yet. Ten years from now, they'll be grateful for what you had done for them."

Always respectful, I would answer, "Please do not placate me or misunderstand me in this."

Actually, some are grateful now. I hear a "thank you" now and then. And, since returning to the classroom, I had been invited to more than a few graduation parties. That pleases me immensely but a few is not all and my concern remains.

Each day, I want to be all that I can be. Each day, I want my effort to make a positive difference leading all to be Good Citizens of Earth.

During a prolonged illness of one daughter, my wife and I

became involved in a support group, Hope For Hearts. We did not have a lot of time to participate but we did read the periodic newsletter. In one was a little poem, *Alabaster Boxes*. The unknown author wrote:

Do not keep the alabaster boxes of your love and tenderness sealed up until your friends are dead.

Fill their lives with sweetness. Speak approving, cheering words while their ears can hear them and while their hearts can be thrilled and made happier by them.

The kind things you mean to say when they are gone, say them before they go.

The flowers you mean to send, use to brighten and sweeten their homes before they leave them.

If my friends have alabaster boxes laid away, full of fragrant perfumes of sympathy and affection, I would rather they would bring them out in my weary and troubled hours and open them, that I may be refreshed and cheered when I need them.

Let us learn to anoint our friends beforehand. Post mortem kindnesses do not cheer the burdened spirit. Flowers cast no fragrance backward over the weary way.

8

On returning final exams on the last day of a school year, a student stopped me at her desk to offer a compliment. That is always appreciated especially when someone is specific.

She said, "Because of the way you teach, how you go about doing things in class, and what you expect from us, I learned to study differently. My grade here shows that. All of my grades are better. Anymore, I don't concentrate on memorization."

No sooner said, then another nearby student who had overheard and with her another student who did not until this time earn outstanding grades confirmed, "You helped me a lot, too."

"How is that?" I replied.

With one nodding approval, the other responded, "I learned in your class. Your class helped me to grow up. I gave up on making flash cards. I don't study using outlines, either. I use my book and class notes. I try to make associations."

Guess. For these students, were their scores on the final exam satisfactory? Did their scores measure up to the state standards for success?

Perhaps they did. Their scores were in the upper seventies to low eighties. Not outstanding but according to them, better than they had done before at least in any of their science classes.

These students as examples believed that their classroom accomplishments were more than just the ability to respond to state standards test questions as important as that is presumed to be. They appeared to have been satisfied with gains that are intangible and not easily quantified.

I wondered, "Is that okay? Should that learning be applauded? Is one more significant and lasting over time? Should we value the ability to learn over the ability to correctly answer all of the questions? Did these students disavow the singular focus on the heretofore all important vocabulary?

They did affirm setting aside the use of flash cards and they did declare having given up on the generally thought to be all important concept limiting outline in preparation for a test.

Did they begin to realize that the use of these "tools" limit the range of study and prohibit seeing enough to understand? Did they start to recognize that these often relied upon study formats are only sketchy descriptors of an assembly of specifics or a fundamental framework representing a complex construct, a meaningful concept? Did they come to appreciate that links and interconnections create the invaluable insights that enable the selection of the most suitable or most correct option from among several? Were they now thoughtful, thinking?

Generally, high school students are unskilled learners. Why should they be other than that?

They are still into "Thumbs Up and Thumbs Down" and the like. They are still playful. They have the raw abilities but they seem not to know how to synthesize their wherewithal into working systems that build or assemble mental configurations that overall maximize the potential for general recall and all important problem solving.

This is where real teaching happens. Helping students learn for themselves so any information on any topic is within their grasp. It is not in a vacuum of right answers but rather in the world of countless thoughts and interrelated records that have been handed down as our heritage. Most of all, it can take them to new places, actually "out of the box." This is the transition that students need to make and this is the true responsibility of teachers and schools, to get them there without limiting external interferences. Each on their own, curiosity can then unfold into new frontiers for discovery and creativity and maybe inventiveness becomes possible.

As I reflect, it is far easier by repetition to "drill" memorization into these very young accepting learners who have little or no recourse. Easily, they are forced into compliance and readily respond to the conditioning.

Ivan Pavlov taught a dog to respond to a bell. That was great for Pavlov. As well, it may have been great for the dog but that is doubtful.

Similarly, in the way of Pavlov, "Ding-a-ling, it's test time."

Is that great for a teacher of youngsters or for the youngsters themselves? Will "factoid" accumulation enable them as they independently go on? What constitutes learning and how should that be properly assessed? Can any satisfaction be derived in the assurance that students will write back on queue what they have been specifically instructed to write down?

All of what is learned can be listed on a rubric of sorts for easy and consistent grading of papers.

Is it "robots" that society needs as a product of teaching?

Actually students that think independently with insights that they have acquired, articulated, and assembled into a new whole or into alternative patterns would be preferred, I believe.

Is it reasonable to contend that developing the foundations for investigation, research, and study leading to the formulation of some solution for some issue or problem whether significant or not should be at least one important goal of education?

Is it okay to ask, "Did teaching occur and did learning take place if students who are taught according to one style given various elements of a concept cannot respond if asked about the concept from another perspective or point of view?"

How much of every concept must be universal before teaching

and learning can be declared? What if some elements are left out by design? Are students less well off for it? What if because of new discoveries, something is added to a course, are teachers not obligated to take something out? Can a container become overfilled? Can disagreement in teaching exist about what is essential and what is not? Should it be tolerated or even permitted?

If students were to be taught what is truly representative, if they were to be taught how to solve genetics problems as Gregor Mendel actually did, using a binomial method that includes the probability of occurrence of possible gene combinations, if then the students by textbook simplifications and state standards were asked to solve genetics problems in a format as accepted by "obedient" teachers are downgraded because they are not familiar with the application of the alternative non Mendelian method, the Punnett square, who is right?

In this case, the commonly professed method is a distortion. Yet, every textbook presents this method and subsequently every teacher does present this approach according to established standards as if it were unquestionably acclaimed authentic, designed by Mendel himself.

Arguing that the alternative method helps students understand is not valid. It is speaking more or less as a former colleague explaining how he teaches technique in graphing, "Count four spaces this way and five that way. Place the point. With a few examples, they get it."

With a smile he continues, "And, does it matter? A few years from now they'll be installing rivets as directed and they'll be making more money than either of us."

It seems that the rightful job of teaching is to simplify whatever is to be learned but not to be misleading in doing so. The ideal is not to present some distortion. Preferred is making "things simple" and then building sensible connections so that concepts can grow.

Similarly, what if the teaching focus is only on the two

fundamental laws of genetics? And, what if the standards test requires that a student list or identify three or four of Mendel's contributions, elaborations that are in the context of the original two? What if a student cannot reconcile the "third or fourth" with the fundamental two? Should the learning be discounted?

At any given time, how much should any student know about variations? And, what if they know of idiosyncrasies that were not included? What if intangible constraints limited the knowledge that they could display? Whose fault is that? Was the teaching inadequate, learning insufficient? Was it that the measuring methods fell short? How was it established that at a given age students should have command, competency, or mastery over "this" rather than "that?" What should be the limits, the range of tolerance?

Realizing that which already has been established may be arguably arbitrary, what if that which is required in teaching and that which is likely achievable may be altogether different realities? Are teachers and schools as mandated by variously designed prescriptions preparing individuals for what is most needed, to be above all, Good Citizens of Earth?

Education may be standing on its head to help students learn but truly it first needs to be standing on its feet. Education unknowingly cannot risk accommodating tradition for the sake of tradition as the young lady cooking the Thanksgiving ham. That is an unacceptable "legacy cost." Educators, the classroom teachers themselves, need to study the problems of education and what really matters in education and begin to pursue those ends. This would be following a "best practices" policy.

Is the outcome of effort acceptable if both teachers and students extend themselves while making room for their individual differences? Should educators be about discovering shortfalls in requirements and systems? Is it reasonable that educators need to design applicable methods, rethink the nature of teaching, and reorganize the school making it enabling as well as accommodating? Is it pragmatic to presume that educators need to understand what reasonably should be learned or can be learned and when or how it can be learned?

Ultimately, if the students are taught well, teachers mostly but the community as well should have the confidence that their students, their children, can on their own at some later time study and learn as may be needed every detail of everything that justifiably may have been left out of a course or the curriculum.

Some time ago, I served as a mentor for a young lady who anticipated a career in teaching high school biology. However, to my dismay, she was clueless in the preparation of media on which to grow bacteria. Moreover, she had little know-how in the preparation of any materials that students might use during their laboratory experiences. Simply, she had no lab set up experience and she did not have the wherewithal to figure it out. Yet, she was trained in a most reputable state university.

This is not a singular experience. I have worked with others who were similarly under prepared. These experiences have led me to question at least some of the authority that had written convoluted standards that need to be unraveled to discern their meaning.

Is it reasonable to question this authority that has failed in its responsibilities of adequately preparing teachers?

Nonetheless, communities are unwilling to hand over the job of structuring education and support the effort of professionals in the trenches, those in the classrooms who absolutely can make a difference.

Today, school systems are offering data training. Yesterday, meaning decades ago, teachers were offered the basics in tests and measurements and training in criterion development, in other words, setting goals and objectives. As well, teachers were offered insights into mastery learning and comprehensive learning styles.

What is the difference between saying “standard” and “goal,” or "indicator" and "objective" or "exemplary" and "mastery?" In effect, the new is the old only in disguise, in the lingo costume of the time. Yet it is bought at great expense hook, line, and sinker as if it were some "fix it" method, the end all of progress that will upgrade the outcomes of the classroom experience. In a few years, will someone come up with some alternative jargon and again present it as a fundamental precept and remedy?

Why are school systems resurrecting that which had been already in their repertoire but now by another name? How did what teachers learned ages ago as beneficial practices get sidelined only to be restored?

In the sequence of events this latest outcropping might be described as "reinventing the wheel" or for some arguably an event in "spinning our wheels" going nowhere.

Should the slate just be wiped clean for a new beginning at the beginning?

Teachers could do it if they were thought to be resourceful and if they were given the opportunity to be creative. However, at the end of the school year, keys to buildings and classrooms have to be returned.

How senseless is that? Where will the development take place in the home basements or garages of teachers without the aid of equipment and materials and at what expense garnered by whom?

The answer for the last question may well be, "Oh, isn't that the responsibility of the teacher? Isn't that part of their job?"

Ask that of any other group of enlisted professionals. The response might be quite different.

Throughout the academic year, teachers as I have found, find themselves so busy with the various aspects of their work coupled with in-service and licensure requirements that they do not have time to develop their courses. During the academic year, some have been found to stay in the building nearly twelve hours a day.

In testimony, my workload required nine to ten hours per day seven days a week including classroom time, assigned "volunteer" responsibilities, and take home work.

Please do not counter with, "Teachers get the summer off."

By the time the summer comes around, many teachers, having worked sixty or more hours per week every school week, have logged in well over one hundred hours more than hourly workers do in twelve months. When school is in session, for any conscientious teacher especially in science, time is limited to the essential classroom required chores.

The contracts with teachers and their compensation packages need to be changed so as to enable all of the work that needs to be done through the year whether school is in session or out of session. The entire school structure needs to be changed so that the "best of teachers" can be utilized so that the outcomes for students can be maximized. Incidentally, the "best of teachers" are those who not only have the academic credentials but also have a knack in shaping students and have the know-how in presenting the heritage so that learning occurs.

With standards now virtually etched in stone, flexibility is prohibited.

With textbooks even providing day-to-day, word-for-word teacher presentations for every class throughout the academic year, will all individuality be replaced?

The textbook publishers without accountability requirements by design or default are gaining more and more control over outcomes. That cannot be right. The individuality of the teacher coupled with their particular and unique insights has to be preserved. The various imposed negative constraints even out of noble intentions have to be removed. Unknowingly, as it is, the system is bringing about a diminished wholesomeness of its most important entity, the student, the one it was intended to serve.

Teaching is at the point where what is to be taught and how it is to be taught has been mandated with the consequence of limiting and curtailing the wonder of individual differences and the differences that can be made in the classroom.

Firsthand, I know the constraints. It is easy to dump, dump, and dump more and more and it is easy to demand, demand, and demand without end but what is the right amount of "what" so that teachers and schools are both efficient and effective?

Really, does anybody know?

I have concluded that it is not as important to be a decorated "blue ribbon" school as it is to be right in doing what is right for the entrusted students. This point of view applies equally to teachers as it does to our schools.

9

At one time, I accepted a teaching assignment that was predicated on the presumptions of a "brain-based learning" approach. The course was an amalgam of chemistry and physics topics, a simplified trade-off for the traditional high school courses of chemistry and physics. This course that combined both sciences was a way out permitting students to graduate with a college admission worthy diploma.

It was a hodgepodge of topics. But, why was it a course of a bit of "this" mixed with a little of "that?" Why something here and some other there? Why not a mix of other representative general topics?

While acceptable, content was a designer bias. Unacceptable was author adamancy.

Aside from the context and disposition, perhaps eyebrows might be raised with concern for a course that proclaims to be predicated upon "brain-based learning." Presume that this is just another example of "jargoneering." A rose by any other name is still a rose.

But, what does "brain-based learning" suppose?

Collectively educators might proclaim several types of learning that certainly involve the brain and obviously are "brain-based." Only recently has this "brain-based learning" been privileged with an obvious title coupled with a definition of sorts. It proposes that learning takes place through designed hands-on activities that will lead students to intended but self-generated conclusions, essentially, "give them directions and afterward let them figure out the 'what' of what they did."

Open for criticism from colleagues, except for one missing part, nothing is new in "brain-based learning" other than the author proclaimed idiosyncrasies. The shortfall is in the presumed presence of student wherewithal to accurately derive associated conclusions.

What truly differentiates the various forms of learning as might be described is not that the brain is or is not involved but rather how the material is presented and how it is ultimately processed and assessed?

Just as well, this teaching method could have been called, "On-Your-Own-Discover-What-Is-Already-Known Learning."

Is this presumptuous? Is this an example of expecting an unfounded outcome, of supposing too much?

In this "brain-based learning" situation, the material being taught through laboratory involvement, in a contextual environment, required students to work in small groups, quasi teams, with the prospect that those so involved would at least collectively arrive at the desired predetermined conclusions.

Was it presumed that a Newton, Archimedes, Maxwell, Arrhenius, Boyle, or Joule would be in their midst ready to postulate the logical inferences or possible deductions?

It did not happen. The students could not do it. They were unable to arrive at the "hoped for" or desired outcomes unless those outcomes were immediately obvious.

For example, students were able to recognize that a model car freely traveling down a ramp would be going faster at the end of the ramp than at the start of the ramp, and on questioning a few would realize that for the car to be going faster at the end at each preceding instant it would have had to go a bit faster. But, none could say, "Oh look, the car is accelerating due to gravity as it going down the ramp as it is inclined." They could not make the connection. They were unfamiliar with rate and rate of change. It was not in their mindset. They could identify a force called gravity but they did not understand or link its impact on the car.

They had to be led along. They would have to be asked, "At what place on the ramp, here, here, or here is the car going fastest and by how much more than at that location or the location before? At each point, what was the rate of change?"

Most unrealistically, based solely on their observations, the students were expected to derive the formula that expressed the rate of change, a formula for acceleration. Likewise, they could not do it. They were not prepared to make all of the needed associations.

Of course, which student might dare to answer for all if asked, "Can you express your observations in some kind of formula?"

They would "duck and hide" with their faces turned downward looking away indicating some kind of disengagement, apathy, or anxiety proclaiming, "How would I know? Please don't call on me. Don't ask me to figure that out to be the goat for all of the others. It would be unfair."

For the higher order conclusions that required associations to be made respectfully, the students just could not make the transition from the situational application to the overriding analytical principle or abstract generalization. They seemed not able to process all of the input and if they could arrive at the intended conclusions, they were concealing the evidence that indicated that they could.

Why would anyone expect that students might go through the required logical sequence of steps except for those who put the "kabobulation" together?

The distance between what they did hands-on and what they were to plausibly conclude was for whatever the reason apparently too great. Only one person concluded the Theory of Relativity after a bicycle ride over the roads of Tuscany. And, only one person, after supposedly seeing an apple fall from a tree, realized the Theory of Gravity.

Consequently, in accommodating the needs of those observers not Einstein-talented or Newton-brilliant, a lot of post lab time was needed. The after-lab dialogs were tedious but it was the only vehicle that intermeshed the various bits of information. Often portions of the laboratory activity were repeated as a demonstration to help in recall, to enrich observation, or prevent detachment as "when will there be an end to this?"

Students saw "things" happening. They could describe what they observed but they were unable to independently or collectively derive what had been desired, drawing the right conclusions, writing the formula that summarized their work.

After a few of these laboratory episodes, it became apparent that students relied solely upon the post laboratory presentation. They knew from past experiences that answers would be provided no matter how well or how poorly they performed or how diligently they attended to observations in the hands-on activity. Some were more conscientious than others but generally, answers were answers and that was all that seemed to matter. The paramount goal was to get the answers somehow from another student or from the post mortem exercise. The possession of answers brought a sense of accomplishment and closure.

Interesting for me was the common student remark of that closure nonchalantly said, "Where do you want my work?"

Having learned, having been equipped with the wherewithal to solve problems was inconsequential. Perhaps immaturity interfered. While most were polite, they seemed to want to get on with the explanation and to be done with it. The impatience might be translated as, "I'm bored. I'd like to have some fun. Going over what we already did is tiring. Can we do something else? I just want my grade." Consequently, the energy of more than a few was funneled into a singular enterprise, getting the answers.

This was disheartening. It was "the empty truck at the loading dock."

Different would be better but how can it become different if the approach is to first do some stuff, then struggle to understand it generally to no avail, and finally to get some answers. Somehow we need to engage students in the kinds of processes that lead to learning that results in independence.

However, the mixture of hands-on ingredients could be organized into a representative conclusion when approached in a Guided Discovery Learning context, an approach that would lead students incrementally bringing about new insights step by step rather than drowning them through total immersion leaving them clueless and dependent.

This procedure of Guided Discovery Learning is used to describe the laboratory sequences set into an individualized instruction format. Students are led to representative conclusions following a pathway of questions each of which being answered with the results of stepwise experiments with each being a simulation of those conducted by the researchers who in their day essentially asked the same questions, followed the same path, and arrived at the same end point. It encourages wonder, the beginning point of creativity.

Presumably, following a precisely laid out innovative path, students would develop thinking patterns in problem solving without the blind alley, pull-the-wool-over-your-eyes, stumped-are-you, see-if-you-can-figure-it-out activities that muddle up the often common teaching/learning process.

Simply, students pursue the answers to questions that emerge from even prompted curiosity that in turn leads to the design of a system that might provide an answer for the question that now leads to another question coupled to an experiment, and so on. With questions followed by explorative work, students are led each step of the way. They are artificially placed into the context of investigators as if doing the research for the first time.

For example, Jean-Baptiste Van Helmont wondered, "What are plants made of?" His conclusion was incorrect but if not water, then from what are plants really made? With the question raised, the follow up could lead to the chemical analysis of plant tissues and from those results stepwise to eventually the chemical reaction for photosynthesis.

While students in the "brain-based learning" environment were hunting answers and while teachers including myself were attempting to lead students to come up with the correct conclusions from their doings, teachers would express frustration in the fruitlessness of effort and students would communicate frustration in their waiting.

Occasionally, as I have worked in and out of classrooms or prep rooms or just by chance walking through a hallway without seeking any input, I would overhear the apprehensive conversations of the "brain-based learning" advocates. Among themselves or on occasion with other teachers, they would express disillusionment with the system that for some reason they continued. One of the faculty members frequently involved in this kind of demoralizing dialog did moonlight as an adjunct university professor.

Often she would complain that many of the students in the university level classes did not measure up to the required level of performance. As a result, as might be expected, this teacher had chosen to ratchet up the requirements in her high school class and asked other chemistry teachers to do the same.

The misguided logic was, "How else would the high school students know enough to succeed at the college level?"

The intentions may have been good but will the outcome best serve the needs of the high school students?

In order for these students at the high school level to get it, the eighth grade science teachers would next be asked to raise their academic bar. This kind of demand more of the students goes down through the system teaching for higher and higher achievements with more requirements so as to be prepared for the next more difficult level.

Could this kind of demand and expectation be

counterproductive? Could this be why students were asked to memorize the periodic table in the seventh grade? Will they be better prepared for their high school encounters? As this goes on, gradually, is the bar raised until it is beyond the reach of at least some if not many of the students, of course all for their benefit? Could this be why some give up and quit?

In effect, is a more elementary level teacher being asked to carry the load for someone up the chain not able to succeed in doing the job they agreed to do? Are younger students being burdened to do more before its time? What will be the consequences of continuously raising the bar? When is enough, enough?

Lest the students become worn out, a policy needs to be implemented that mandates "If something is added, something must be taken out." At least with this imposition, teachers, chairpersons, curriculum directors, and even principals would have to give some thought before burdening the curriculum with even more content. How much can a student reasonably learn in a reasonable amount of school time? Does anyone know?

When serving on the curriculum improvement committee of a small college, the nursing department continued to add course after course, more and more work to the curriculum. Surely, nurses needed to know the mix of material but over time the two-year degree required three years for completion. In effect, the graduates of the program were not receiving proper recognition for their work.

Can this be justified?

These righteous faculty members were behaving badly as perhaps some little league parents do in demanding more and more in performance but of course, demanding of others not demanding of themselves.

After pointing out this discrepancy during a committee meeting, I was reprimanded. Subsequently, I fell into disfavor with the nursing faculty. My position would be unwavering. Get it right for the student. In this example, a sixty-four credits college degree padded with thirty extra hours is still a two-year degree. The students may know more. They may be better equipped with knowledge. But, they have earned only the Associates degree. If they need the additional information, change the degree to match up with the requirements.

In all of this, expectations are paramount. What we impose upon students is at the forefront. That needs to be realistic.

A series of discussions with associate graduate students was the decided upon starting point for designing instruction. These initial discussions led to a series of scheduled meetings with groups of undergraduate students and associate graduate students. The focus was to find out what the undergraduate students believed to be important issues that needed to be covered in a general studies biology course tempered with what was thought to be the essential and basic principles of biology.

Once a week over the course of an academic year, five to eight undergraduate students in response to an invitation offered to participate in these dialogs that lasted about one hour rarely two hours. From time to time, departmental professors attended. After what the many students said was important to them, it became our job as teachers, mostly mine as the lead course writer, to figure out how their ideas could be structured into a worthy presentation that as well represented the generally acknowledged constructs and fundamental topics. Essentially, this was the substance of the starting point summed up as the needs assessment.

This kind of participation does have to take place at some time early on to establish the baseline of reference for the to-be-fabricated course.

Understand that the key is input, input from every possible source. The leadership group had to be confident that everyone that needed to be involved was brought into the project. It was critical that everyone had the feeling that their input was important and that they had a real stake in the project. With this philosophy, all were willing to do whatever it took to realize the highest possible level of success.

Looking back, I asked several questions of myself, "Is the final work thoughtful? Is wholesome consideration given to each of the recommended elements? Is it workable and achievable? Does the strategic plan for implementation with all inherent parameters and concerns honestly include the contributions, issues, and justifications of every partner in the enterprise? Will the overall endeavor be purposeful? Will the plan satisfy the Law of Minimums, making possible at least the most noteworthy outcomes without yielding to the superficial? Ultimately, will the achieved work be worthwhile and meaningful?

It is essential to look not at the bottom line that defines minimum student performance and school success by the number of individuals who achieved at or beyond some arbitrary level such as sixty or seventy per cent but rather to check into the accomplishment of individuals throughout the population.

It was necessary to ask, "How did each individual student do? Was it at his or her level, below or above? How was each student affected as determined by correlation to some pre-established datum point? Did each student end up better off because of something they experienced by design compared possibly with where they might have ended up without intervention?"

Considering all that has been set forth by state directives, was sufficient dialog provided accommodating the to-be-affected individuals? Were marketplace surveys conducted? Were teachers involved? Were students considered? Were all on board from the onset and throughout the needs assessment process?

With the establishment of evaluation tools, was every possibility considered? Was baseline data gathered? Were reference points identified? Were acceptable outcomes defined or did the process progress exclusively, arbitrarily, and haphazardly?

Given what is, what if the mandated evaluation instruments had a pertinent section consisting of eight items? What if the overall score for all of the enrolled students was just less than fifty per cent? Was an analysis conducted on the items to determine their cognitive level: knowledge, comprehension, application, analysis, synthesis, or evaluation? What if three of the items were higher order requiring more than a typical knowledge platform? With that new consideration, was the student performance acceptable realizing that lower scores might be quite satisfactory if higher order attainment was required?

Higher scores are rightfully expected for knowledge level or trivia type items.

Most of all, the pitfall of presuming that open ended questions are inherently linked to higher order cognition must be avoided. Caution here! Often open ended questions requiring an essay response can be presented with just a series of knowledge level statements. This should be evident from the common scoring chart that typically is developed to assure objectivity.

Does an acceptable response to an open ended question represent significant learning?

If after comprehensive evaluation of achievement as measured overall is different or skewed from that which was desired, then, what?

Perhaps the entire project will have to be reevaluated.

Is the leadership team prepared to scrap the project and begin anew? Or, because of all the investment, will they twist and turn the outcome data to get a false but preferred outcome? In this, are they not "tempting" reality? Is that not the ultimate test, being honest with results that would set in motion a round of improvements?

Perhaps only an adjustment of standards or prescribed criteria will be sufficient, rethinking the outcomes of the original needs assessment.

In projects such as these, the role of each individual and every teacher needs to be prescribed and defined very much like the role of each player on basketball or hockey teams. Reasonably, none should contribute randomly. None should have a self-determined role. In their role, the work of each individual involved including the teachers should be assessed. Role descriptions are essential. This should be agreeable.

It must be kept in mind that whatever the project, all aspects of it ought to be quantifiable and referenced to some specific objective and its potential sub parts. In particular, the test instruments need to be inclined toward the rigors of statistical analysis. Variables need to be identified, isolated, and evaluated.

In all of this, documentation is required. Notes need to be kept that summarize each step along the way from onset to conclusion. It is imperative to have decided up front what it is that needs to be achieved. Only after meeting these prerequisites can students be appropriately prepared for that achievement, at some expressed level of learning. Then, and only then, can a performance criteria based evaluation instrument become meaningful and take form.

This process requires a lot of demanding attention to detail. It is a lot of work. It takes a lot of time to do it right.

While schools and school systems may not be fully prepared for the rigors of required accountability, certainly teachers ought to be as a part of their undergraduate training. An unintended though fortuitous alternative outcome of accrediting agency imposed measures may be the authentic development of teaching through the use of general self-assessment and personal accountability tools. The foundation for change may well be in place. Only follow-up may be needed.

As they enter the profession, teachers should be fortified with expertise in their particular academic disciplines and they should have some substantive insights in subject matter presentation as well as student management. However, their efforts should be augmented with the basic wherewithal enabling the critical examination of their work and its impact reflected by the progress of students. Teachers as acting individuals or as members of a team should understand and be equipped to apply fundamentally as well as significantly critical and indispensable statistical tools. Teachers working independently or in association with others should be prepared in the utilization of basic test and measurements analysis.

Above all, teachers should be able to understand and calculate test item difficulty. If appropriate information technology systems are not available, teachers need to be able to set up a simple spreadsheet grid that will permit a tally of the number of correct and incorrect responses for each student by question.

The question difficulty is determined by adding the tally marks of the students for each question. A rule might be established that knowledge level questions must be examined if fewer than seventy per cent of the students can correctly respond. For comprehension level questions, perhaps at least sixty per cent should correctly respond. Of course, these breaks are arbitrary. Certainly, the higher order of cognition that is required fewer students can be expected to respond correctly in all aspects.

If questions are too easy, they are less useful in discriminating among students for placement into grade categories but more importantly, they are less revealing in instructional development. By thoughtful analysis of objectives, a "right" mix of questions can be developed for the discernment of achievement and grade ranking.

However, if students have difficulty in responding correctly to any item, necessarily, the problem is not with the question, its wording and options, but may reflect a need for a teaching method alteration. It may be a combination of several elements. If records that associate teaching methods and elements with objectives including the proposed cognitive achievement level are kept, teaching efficiency and effectiveness may be reliably linked. In other words, if "this" then "that" can be an expected result or outcome.

Once, while in graduate school, a videotape had been prepared to instruct students in the study of the chick embryo. During the laboratory period, the videotape player malfunctioned. As a backup, a 35 millimeter slide series was in place.

After review, it was discovered that students understood the chick embryo related process more completely using the still shot series. Indeed, this was a lesson learned. What sometimes is thought to be better, more attractive, or artistic may in reality be less effective as a teaching tool. Consider the options. Surprises do happen in teaching.

In addition, a reliability coefficient should be calculated to provide confidence that a test instrument, again structured to be congruent with the objectives, is accurately measuring some characteristic of the student population taking the test. A high coefficient would mean that individual test items are producing corresponding patterns of response among similar student groups and in general are valid.

The application of at least these statistical tools will enable teachers to intimately become involved in the design and development of instructional strategies and systems. Thus, teachers will be enabled to evaluate every element within their instructional plan and as a result make knowledgeable and deliberate adjustments that lead to overall teaching improvement.

Working within a set of constructs, they will be able to assess the all important efficiency and effectiveness of selected presentation methods and techniques without the force of some external intimidation. They will be able to watch over themselves. They will know firsthand how well they are doing and may gain insights into their effort and the effort of students. Ideally, they will be able to share their findings with others in the profession enabling all to advance the frontier. Schools should provide vehicles as journals or other publications that specifically extend this opportunity.

With some tools for statistical analysis of test results, a recognition of various levels of cognition, and the ability to write objectives that focus on the most essential and valued subject area concepts, teachers can begin to thoughtfully and systematically design, implement, and refine instruction. A number of assorted questions can be examined that progress through a course of study.

Some queries might include: Was the test reliable and generally valid? Were test questions congruent with the objectives? Was question difficulty at an appropriate level? Were the corresponding presentations and instructional sequences appropriate for achieving the objectives?

Predicated upon reliable data, teachers can make purposeful adjustments achieving more and more perfection in their work while enhancing learning. As teachers become involved in their own accountability, quality control, and analysis of instructional design, they can become masterful in the practice of teaching.

11

Every day the objective for the day, now controlled by some aspect of a prescribed standard, has to be conspicuously posted or distributed. So, I was told by a principal.

The ritual is, "Tell them what you are going to tell them before you begin to tell them." The practice is reasonable. Not so explicable is the terminology as applied in connection with learning.

Why standard rather than "goal?" Is "standard" something borrowed from industry evoking quality with the belief that the use of the term will render a desirable outcome more than otherwise?

In life, most people understand the terms, goal and objective. Reasonably, everyone sets goals and has objectives to achieve. However, jargon in education, likely an inadvertent attempt at securing a professional vocabulary seems to prevail rather than focus upon substantive accomplishment. It seems that by altering language means and ends will be transfigured into some positive and that subsequently the sought after outcomes are assured.

Really is it a tactic of make believe? Is setting a standard something more than establishing a goal? Seriously, will the use of standard instead of goal lead to accomplishment in the classroom?

What needs to be realized is that results are not predicated upon a descriptive word or phrase but rather on purposeful classroom transactions often the combination of operational skills, interest imperatives, and assorted intangibles.

However, this procedure of posting objectives extracted from whatever the preference, standards or goals, can be a savior heading off conflicts as when parents inquire about the success of their daughter or son. Thoughtfully designed or not, with these all important statements identified by whatever term is in vogue, a teacher always is better positioned even in response to administrative inquiries and evaluations about job performance.

Teachers can proclaim, "Look here! These were the points for focus, the essentials of what was being presented, what was to be studied and learned. The students did not do their job in response."

With these intended outcomes before the students, it may be thought that at least some of the responsibility is shifted now onto the student. Of course, that is not so. Learning has always been seen as predicated upon teaching and thus, if learning cannot be verified, the fault though incorrectly rests with the teaching. Always, without substantive justification, accountability is associated with the teacher.

In bemoaning this issue, I was given the proverb, "When the mind is ready, a teacher appears."

In any case, learners do need to have a perspective of what they will be learning. That may ready the mind. Objectives then may provide for both purpose and direction. Ideally, they would serve as guidelines as well as mile markers along a guided journey.

Regrettably, in practice, objectives used to support teaching often lead to dreaded shortfalls: the teaching of "factoids" from a narrow band of selected information and the pursuit of minutiae leading to the pit of coveted answers.

Without consideration, teachers and students less stringently are being held responsible for only a narrow band of superficial or frivolous learning of questionable usefulness even if valued at parties or quiz shows. The use of objectives should provide for much more.

Rather than just serve as guidelines for teaching and learning, would it not be better if objectives were constructed to stepwise lead students to higher order learning, abilities and skills, such as understanding or analysis and even curiosity that absolutely must be preserved in the context of all the learning outcomes? Should the overriding goal be to seek the best of all?

Years ago, when I first entered into teaching, students would eagerly ask, "What do I have to know?"

Facetiously, I would answer, "Everything that is presented."

For them though it may not have been a common practice, the "key points" for every topic always had been distributed, a copy handed to every student. The "What To Know" page as students had called it was not in the form of a list or an outline because either of the configurations would have had the inherent potential leading to academic self-destruction, studying and learning the skeletal components. Rather, the distributed sheet was organized with annotations supported with references to textbook pages including figures and captions that represented significant interrelated information that merited thoughtful examination. Perhaps it could be described as an instruction driven concept map.

In addition to the "take notice" elements, the statements representing what might then have been called objectives made available a structure for student note taking while "telling" them what will follow and where they will end up. Come along on the journey and be interactive. The "What To Know" hand out, never more than one side of a single sheet, enabled the integration of parts or facets into the formation of big ideas or models. It was a kind of point by point summary, an ordered sequence enabling emergence of the intended composite.

From this perspective, the student "What To Know" document was a helpful tool in assisting students in learning how to learn as well as being a useful structure for developing congruent evaluation instruments that could "tell" student and teacher to what extent learning had progressed. Post test review with the students always included reference to the "What To Know" items.

Secondly, for me it afforded a tool for reflection whether or not the employed teaching strategies intended to solicit a learning effort were effective. The elements of presentation notes were analyzed as part of a progression driving improvement.

Basically, the "What To Know" structure presented a higher order platform for the redesign of instructional methods enabling the removal of defects and the enhancement of techniques leading to ever increasing classroom effectiveness and learner efficiency. It served as the foundation for a teacher "lessons learned" journal.

Did the classroom illustrations, examples, references, materials, and activities achieve the primary teacher intentions? What was the contribution of each definable component?

Reflecting upon those early efforts, I am pleased because when I started out in teaching, I had been literally clueless reacting to circumstances. My philosophy was simple, "Do again what worked. Give up on what did not."

Going back to the beginning after venturing off with a side step to the "What To Know" sheet and its merits, here and there the ordered must-be-on-the-board objectives certainly derived from mandated standards indeed have inherent marginal limits.

While value is seen in the eyes of the beholder, over concerned with the typical knowledge acquisition centered constructs useful in differentiating between the artificial categories of competency and mastery or empowered and proficient, objectives are being perceived as a kind of end all in the classroom.

Useful as they are, the presentation of objectives is only a relatively small part of a totality that makes up the instructional design process. As required in the classroom, they represent only one aspect in the measurement of capability and accomplishment.

It may be well to note that the objectives as commonly required in their most basic and most fundamental form however made available to the student posted or distributed are an adjunct resource linked to some paramount purpose or intent. They represent the tip of the proverbial iceberg in education. They are only an outcome or derivative of the underlying instructional need to teach prescribed matters including proposed methods of exchange and interactive dialogs as well as perhaps an assortment of vehicles for meaningful teacher self-evaluation and accountability. They emerge only from the instructional development procedure that is the interrogative supported pre assessment tool focused upon a discernable and justifiable need for "this" rather than "that" knowledge or know-how.

Note, the encumbering standards as prescribed likely founded without adequate research require dissection often by committee for disjunction of paramount needs and teachable objective elements. They are more like what "we would like to see accomplished generally" rather than "this is what has to be achieved definitively." Rather than applaud and accommodate the work, those who developed the standards need to be challenged.

Why were the standards written so as to be discretionary requiring interpretation? Will the various deciphering committees or individuals be consistent in the extraction process coming up with the same objectives so that all students will be similarly taught achieving the standard intended outcomes?

The effort needs to craft two kinds of objectives clearly recognized and necessarily differentiated: for the student to assist learning and for the teacher in anticipation of the configured instructional methodology with associated evaluation devices. As well, the flip side or counterpart to the exacting objectives for the students and teachers are those less tangible outcomes.

As a consequence, will the student be enabled in learning to learn, acquire higher order mental processing skills, and associate outcomes with other disciplines? Will teachers enhance teaching skillfulness and become more involved in professional and collegial associations sharing research and findings?

Agreeably, sequenced objectives in education are needed. Teaching and learning by their very nature and essence imply their purposefulness. It is self evident that randomly achieved end points are only acceptable for aimlessly wandering individuals. Without a set of paramount directives by default any instructional system, any teaching, and any learning will do.

Whatever it is worth, the common teacher appraisal form does include a check box pertaining to the posting, presentation, or distribution of objectives. If these statements are provided at the beginning of a topic of study or if they at least are presented for the scheduled work of the week or other time segment that is good. If not, teacher performance deductions are to be expected.

Overall, while that may seem acceptable, most likely, the box "overlooks" what is at least equally applicable to the teacher, their part of the equation, their focus and their end points derived from the overall instructional design process. However, teachers are not likely to be so involved because their role is reduced to "carry out the task as assigned."

Teachers do need to know at the onset the principal instructional marketplace driven goals. It is primary atop a hierarchy followed by supporting secondary and even tertiary objectives. It is these overriding constructs that lead to the specifically defined student "What To Know" page as might be acceptable.

Clearly, at the starting point must be a thorough and definitive needs assessment sorting first then prioritizing among the identified apparently essential objectives real requirements that are seen to advance the collective welfare as well as real life essentials of the students and all of the environmentally and socially interacting components.

Educators truly need to absolutely know what it is that they are attempting to accomplish before they can design the route, implement the pathway, evaluate progress, and make subsequent adjustments as may become needed progressing to the proverbial summit, the goal. This task is indeed tedious and is much more than the mere presentation of textbook extracted material to presumed "listening" students or a captive audience that is required to write and keep notes.

Does evidence spring forth that suggests this method of needs assessment was foremost in the establishment of state standards?

Determinations must be made on the basis of real data gathering rather than on hearsay or assumed to be worthy points of interest as perhaps state standards are. Perhaps writers of those state standards should have begun with a thorough review and examination of a spectrum of notable requirements from local to global looking into every conceivable nook and cranny and sampling every element of society. As they are, many of the standards are a tangle and each must be resolved yet without certainty that the intended if worthy mark will be hit. Because of their typically overwhelming nature, some from among all must be deemed as more worthy labeled "power" standards that have to be without reservation fitted into the constraints of an academic year.

Why select this one rather that one? What is the value of those not deemed to be "power" standards? Should effort be put forth to present only those "power" standards and to what extent and in deference to what? Does anybody really know?

The application of objectives for teaching and learning emerged in the early 1970's. Their use in education was adopted from the demonstrated usefulness of goal driven processes in industry. They enabled a connection with the elements of Benjamin Bloom's Cognitive Taxonomy presented in the 1950's. While that bit of history may not matter, it does provide some perspective.

As applied, a criterion objective required three elements: 1) the desired outcome needs to be specified, 2) the conditions or situation has to be described, and 3) the frequency of attained accuracy must be noted. Thus, objectives enable defining what it is that needs to be accomplished, how the accomplishment will be demonstrated, and the regularity of the accomplishment: occasional, often, or always.

Carefully articulated for classroom use, objectives must be considered as the essential ingredient, the fundamental framework upon which teaching and learning are predicated. They can be most meaningful in that they are designed to specify the intricacy of each moment of classroom work and define the essential parameters as well as involvements while looking to the overall destination of a topic and the course. They are absolutely necessary in establishing the platform of congruence between teaching and learning. They are critical in the statistical establishment of reliability in the classroom. And, they are significant in the continuous improvement cycle of instructional design and teaching that leads to learning for basic competency and ultimate mastery or at least some level of acceptable performance.

Setting aside shortfalls in use, student answer-seeking and teacher merit appraisal, objectives clearly point out the direction and definitely assist in providing those check points leading to a pre-determined end. Unlike the state standards in their presentation, they do limit and restrict the scope of the subject matter. They are inflexible and would require adjustment should a classroom need arise as some subtlety may have to be advanced.

Overall, the task is to propose objectives not as some kind of safeguard but rather as a reliable route "map" or as a series of guideposts from some starting point "here" to some destination "there" as determined by a serious needs exploration.

Is it permissible to stray from the map, add or delete as you go without the consequence of penalty?

The imperative is that the stated objectives establish a benchmark of expectations, a means of self-assessment for student and teacher alike that is paramount and unfortunately usually overlooked.

12

Once the classroom door is closed, who really knows what goes on, the level at which a course is taught or the real level at which learning is achieved? How much of this seriously is taken to heart by the assigned teachers? Are some more empathetic than others and endearingly inflate grades, too? Are some more rigid and inflexible in their imposed requirements? Could a given teacher in reality, by design or inadvertently, require more or less of students so that a course taught by one teacher may in reality exceed the level of performance required of a course taught by another teacher? Which of the teachers merits the higher regard?

In particular, I recall having with great disenchantment earned a "D" grade in undergraduate Quantitative Analysis I. I had missed a "C" grade by less than one tenth of a point. My per cent score as I may never forget was 76.92.

Prof. Born said, "Sorry. Others will interpret your grade in terms of the reputation of this university."

Truly, I wonder if that ever happens. I would guess that seldom a person tempers what they see on a transcript with, "Oh, a subpar grade from an excellent school, understandable," and then allows the maximum accommodation.

After considerable pleading on several occasions, Prof. Born did agree to reevaluate my laboratory work. However, by then I had become so disheartened with both the prolonged dialog and my letter grade that I had given up on any consideration and trashed all of the notes and lab write-ups for the class. I was out of luck.

Though of little consolation, I did earn a bona fide "C" grade in Quantitative Analysis II. While the professor had a pronounced accent that caused some frustration in following along with his presentations, the laboratory was outfitted with electronic balances that gave quick accurate values. They were unlike the "classic" analytical pan balances that for me anyway produced unreliable measurements, measurements that were essential for the calculations that made up a considerable part of the first semester lab grade. This single advantage resulted in an average improvement of nearly ten per cent. Conditions and circumstances do make a difference.

Of course, some of the difficult circumstances that may be encountered can be avoided. Making in class adjustments on test scores and curving grades fix a lot of problems. For this to occur with some integrity, the teacher has to be introspective and accommodating.

Do tough grading schools always have unrelenting tough grading teachers? Do schools with broader grading scales have easy grading teachers?

Who knows what the ratios might be in the various schools. Teachers within any given system have issues while others do not.

Frankly, I tend to allow for any doubt. I consider myself rather easy in grading but even handed believing that a higher score rather than a lower one is more likely to motivate a student. However, I do not have any data to support that point of view. Generally, I would rather err on the side of mercy. As I believe, the fullness of justice can be invoked at a later date.

Accordingly, do students who earn a fifty per cent score on a test always flunk?

A fifty per cent score on a test if it is the highest score in the class is most likely fudged to be at least a ninety per cent, an "A-" grade or maybe better with sufficient excuses offered for the adjustment.

What is happening here? Is this kind of action an excuse for a poor performance or deplorable test outcome? Does it matter? Is not any alteration of any score distorting the system or any system? Is not at least some ownership required?

Absolutely! If examined in light of data analysis methods, a teacher might discover that the test instrument was seriously flawed. Now, legitimate justification can be made for the considerations according to that analysis.

On the other hand, is a measured tweak permissible to cover inadequate student performance? Might the course content be out of reach for the students or teaching out of alignment?

Perhaps rather than these justifications, consideration should be given to expanding the grading scale to accommodate a wider distribution of scores rather than dealing with a tightened scale as I had experienced as an undergraduate student. Amending scores would not be an issue.

It seems logical if the purpose of a grading scale is to properly place students into a category that represents performance. Indeed, this can be more accurately accomplished if for example the per cent score ranges of 100 to 80, 79 to 60, etc. were used for corresponding categories, "A," "B," etc. It is obviously easier to slot a student into a range of twenty points rather than one of only seven points or even the customary ten points. Teachers would have more latitude in testing without having to fix results to fit into arbitrarily narrow ranges with the level of test questions ranging from knowledge through synthesis.

Narrow or broad, often enough student efforts fall into undesirable categories. All would like to have a better overall score that translates into a better grade. Teachers frequently fall for it. Students expect it. The story goes something like this.

A student with a glum beaten down look seeks sympathy. The individual is excessively polite, cautious, and fumbling for words. Every action seems to be predicated upon a wish for some accommodation.

The student says, "Mrs. Good, I noticed that my grade is an 'F' actually a fifty-seven per cent. Is there anything that I can do to bring it up?"

Now, giving the correct response that is "No!" Mrs. Good comes off looking as cruel and heartless.

Trying to be at least understanding, Mrs. Good responds, "What do you propose?"

Eyes sparkling, the student leaps at the possibility by asking, "Is there some extra credit work that I could do?"

Now, the correct response to this question should be, "Why? You have not done the real work at hand. How can you propose to do something extra?"

Alternatively, should the student ask instead for some outside work, the answer should be, "Why? You have not done the inside work."

Under the circumstances and not to upset a pretty pathetic appearing childish face, Mrs. Good caves in with either, "Give me a day to think about it" that gives hope to the student resulting in a kind of smile coupled with a brightened look of limited excitement or Mrs. Good says, "Answer all of the questions on page thirty-eight due tomorrow" that gives some reserved delight shrouded with a sting recognizing "that's a lot of work for just a few points."

Nonetheless, the student response while positive and enthusiastic is somewhat tempered with restraint, just audibly saying, "I'll have it on your desk tomorrow before school ends. Thank you."

The answering of questions on page thirty-eight proportionally impacts the scores of other students who were not given the opportunity. What is given to one should be proposed to all.

So, should Mrs. Good go before the class saying, "I have decided to give Geraldine an opportunity to improve her grade? The assignment given is to answer all of the questions on page thirty-eight. Should any of you decide to do this, you will be able to improve your grades as well."

At least, some consistency is instituted and students have an option to take advantage of an opportunity. However, Mrs. Good has invited a lot of extraordinary work for herself. And, without a thought perhaps, a "B" level student can acquire an "A" grade status. A distortion exists here that is definitely misleading.

What if instead of, "Answer all of the questions on page thirty-eight" that may relate to something of importance in the course, the student were told to make a scrapbook of ten newspaper clippings on pollution in waterways in the county or Broadway shows in New York City?

At first this seems okay but the student's grade is no longer consistent with the description of the course that makes no reference to collecting newspaper clippings as a part of the content. The course for this student has been changed from the expected vehicles of learning to include a means for bolstering grades that may not include any learning at all. Clipping articles has little to do with reading them, interpreting them, and incorporating them into a knowledge bank of sorts.

In one class, students were permitted to improve their scores by redeeming "good attendance coupons" worth as much as ten points. This seems to be a most egregious violation of grade integrity.

Is good attendance a justification for grade inflation?

Oh, please!

Questionable rewards may be a technique in the management of behavior but as I had discovered, granting coupons that also could be traded for one hour of sleep during class is absolutely wrong.

Such a certificate was found in the notebook of one of my students. Some may consider that an intriguing possibility.

However, that is an absolutely unacceptable teacher technique. It should never be given "clever status" for any reason.

For example, out of one thousand points in the course if that many were available, the ten points represents one per cent of the grade. What is the grade inflation over eighteen weeks even if the student only cashes in on six weeks of perfect attendance, on time and in the seat when the bell rings or tone sounds?

In this case, the grade inflation will be six per cent added to a total score possibly changing a letter grade from failing to passing or a "B" grade to an "A" grade. How will that affect the G.P.A.? How reliably is the performance of this student represented?

Indeed, this is a rank misrepresentation. Grade inflation by whatever the route is never appropriate. It creates a distortion of true worth. Students need to do the work before them. They need to do the work because it has been established as purposeful in contributing to their learning, the development of essential insights. Some teachers do manage to avoid deception from grade inflation by insuring that the students most likely to seek this kind of intervention are not in their classes.

Shortly after completing work on a Master of Arts degree in science education, I went to work in a school with students who were expected to place modestly to well above the average. The teaching assignment was great, five sections of regular biology with several teachers helping to teach an additional section or two. The school had only one teacher assigned to both chemistry and physics.

The progression was obvious. All of the freshman students in the school signed up for biology. Less than one half of those went on to enroll in chemistry and a small fraction of those enlisted in physics.

The reputation of this teacher was well known throughout the school, "Unless you are a genius or near genius, stay out of chemistry and especially do not sign up for physics."

Certainly, this is in contrast to what students should encounter, the encouragement to go on and experience as much academic diversity as their schedule will permit. This is the fiduciary responsibility of every teacher, enabling students to succeed.

In contrast, this teacher had made more importance of himself than of the students. He had by design or unknowingly positioned his courses beyond the reach of most. He made their academic pursuit so difficult that with the exception of biology, students were in effect driven out of the sciences.

Where but in a necessarily accommodating high school environment would these students have the opportunity to learn about the fundamentals of chemistry and physics?

What this teacher had accomplished was wrong for any given reason. Students should be enabled to smell all of the flowers along the academic path so as to develop a broad experience base that would enable good career choices and just practical well-being. Education is about the journey not necessarily the destination. Consequently, with a few exceptions, the number of students in biology ought to be equal to the number of students enrolled in chemistry and equal to the number in physics.

Does this sort of thing happen in other areas for example: the humanities, mathematics, language arts, or music?

The tendency to make “things” harder with student progress through school should be set aside for the determination to help those of the next generation prepare for their individual futures and the contributions they may ultimately make. The only purpose, the primary mission of every school, is to make those essential positive contributions that lead to the development of marketplace-ready Good Citizens of Earth.

13

The final exam considered by most to be a comprehensive overview of a course is the most perplexing educational tool commonly used to certify acquired knowledge. As such, it is representative and limited to some fraction or percentage of the overall grade for course performance.

In contrast, could it be the "last" exam of a series?

As the last exam, it would be one of several. As such it would be less challenging and more manageable. Ideally, this arrangement should become the standard practice.

Over ten years, what is the real difference between knowledge confirmed by examination at the end of the first week compared with that certified at the end of the sixteenth week?

The time difference is only about three per cent.

Consequently, does it matter if a periodically administered exam, a quasi final exam, is given at the end of the second week, fourth week, eighth week, or any week between the first and last? Is a time difference of three per cent as good as it needs to be? Does an end of the course final assure more than any periodic exam?

Not likely. Its impact is somehow always proportional. However, the comprehensive final examination can be presented as an awesome instrument that has inordinate chilling power with the potential to sort among learners and categorize the effort of teachers. Ramifications of this approach should be judiciously considered from anxiety on the one extreme to disregard on the other.

As a rigorous tool of qualification, the comprehensive final examination must measure up. It must be certifiably worthy absolutely representative of every aspect of the meaningful course content. It cannot fall short in any of its presumed and anticipated intentions. Without compromise it must be so constructed that this perceived as most important of all tests will be beyond doubt absolutely and certainly valid and reliable. Of course, this can be excruciatingly difficult. Getting it so very right is not easy.

For all that this may entail, really what does it accomplish?

The following are examples that hopefully will substantially weaken if not dispel any importance that may be attached to or associated with an all inclusive final exam.

One such poorly contrived exam included a section of thirty multiple-choice questions. Today, "multiple-choice" is perhaps called by another name thanks to the "jargoneers." Of those "multiple-choice" criterion-type questions, four required an answer that was associated with seven text pages scattered among just over five hundred pages that were to be covered during the two terms of the course. Approximately, ten times the emphasis was given to this single topic.

Why?

Would any test taker have prepared so disproportionately? Even with all of the scoring precautions and assurances that are commonly in place, is this kind of final examination reasonable or more importantly is it fair?

Another across the board final exam that would count for as much as twenty per cent of the test taker final grade focused on one chapter out of twenty-one that were to have been studied. Eight out of the fifty questions were about material from a single chapter that was composed of about half as many pages as any of the other seventeen chapters.

Is this representative? Is it realistic? Is the selected chapter a preference or a special interest of the test writer?

Anyone can do the math on this.

Obviously, it is biased but why? Was it out of neglect or by design?

The most mind boggling defect was noted in a so-called comprehensive final examination of one hundred items that all students were required to pass demonstrating competency before their completion of a course could be certified. An item analysis revealed that the correct answer was selected most of the time. However, if the correct response were not chosen, the students consistently chose the same incorrect option of the three foils.

My thought was, "That is so remarkable, really amazing. How could that be?"

Clearly, the two out of three foils never chosen had to have been so out of alignment with the demand of the question that neither was ever considered by any student not even the most incompetent. Essentially, the exam was "True or False" masked as multiple-choice with little doubt about what was to be selected as the "True" item.

What can be concluded, that learning occurred, that teaching was at least adequate, that schools were doing their job, and that no child had been left behind? What?

Ah, with a high rate of passing scores, it could be perceived that no child was left behind. The school was applauded, certified for the accomplishment, and recognized as a mastery learning visitation site. However, it achieved the award by deception, an example of "fake" testing. Likely, the students were being groomed and really were not measuring up to ideals as might be conceived. It is the reason why some students only apparently succeed when in reality they still fall short in making the grade.

A common practice among some final exam givers is to make available a "practice final exam" rather than provide a summary of the representative essentials. That is a noble gesture and most likely works out fine but at least in one instance the outcome was disheartening.

The so-called "practice final exam" given to students completing the second term of a course covered material from both first and second semesters. Surely, it was intended to be the "absolute" comprehensive final exam evaluating and confirming the overall abilities and accomplishment of students over the entire school year.

Is that acceptable?

Presume that the "practice final exam" was truly representative and acceptable. Know that in reality, over several days, every item would be explored in detail. Conscientious students and even the involved teachers invested considerable energy in the review process. However, the actual final exam was not at all like the "practice final exam" that had been made available. The emphasis of the given final examination was upon the work of the first term, the most distant subject matter. Surprisingly, the students showed no signs of concern indicating that this was not atypical, being prepared for one configuration and subsequently being tested over another.

Why not more emphasis on the work of the most immediate term or at least a more even distribution?

The material of the first term had been previously tested at the end of the first term.

With a few mismatch experiences as that, most probably, students can be expected to become non believers in the system. Their very good intentions and the ideal accompanying derivatives of a well prepared experience can no longer be valid and supportable.

The attitude of many students toward final exams can be understood, "Why bother. You have no chance. You can't win at this."

What about the student who successfully completed the first

term of the course then for good reason interrupted the continuity and continued with the second term sometime later? What if a year elapsed between taking the first and second semester course segments? Even with an intensive review given that the rate of forgetting may be quite rapid, how much should this individual be expected to remember from the first semester? Because of the academic hiatus, should the individual be given any measure of compensation?

Now with certainty, in anticipation of subsequent answers, many questions still need to be asked.

Can any importance be assigned to certifying exams or classroom final exams especially as those just described as fundamentally skewed? Is a second term course final examination valid if it concentrates on first term concepts? Was the second semester material of lesser stature than that of the first semester? Was the substance of the course concentrated in the first term rather than evenly distributed including the second term?

If significant subject matter were equally spread throughout the course, then would an asymmetric test shortchange the disregarded second term material? So, what did this second term final exam weighted at twenty per cent of the final grade really represent?

Why should students have to deal with a distorted final exam anyway? What does it substantiate? On merit, what relative value should be assigned to it, twenty per cent of the final grade or something other? Should a final exam grade ever replace in part or totality a grade earned throughout a course?

Some teachers with extended prerogatives do assign a course grade equal to that of the final exam grade if it exceeds the accumulated course grade.

When I had been preparing to return to graduate school, in anticipation of courses in physical chemistry, I needed to take calculus, two semesters of it. I signed up at the community campus of a state university. The classes met two times per week for two hours each meeting.

Throughout the course, I struggled earning only a "C" grade on occasional chapter tests. As the course progressed, finally after much tenaciousness, associations were made. I began to understand what needed to be understood.

On the final examinations for first and second semesters, I respectively scored a ninety-two per cent and a ninety-six per cent. The promise of the professor was, "Earn an 'A' on the final and you will have an 'A' for the course. A final grade of "A" was in fact assigned for each semester of my work.

At the time, it seemed fair and even now it seems fair only because every element of the course was needed for success in solving the various examination problems. For courses as this, the destination appears to be as important as the journey. Some might be inclined to argue to the contrary. However, all seems to be justifiable given the nature of the material covered in the course.

As is, the final exam conundrum continues.

Even at twenty per cent of the final grade, students with a course average of seventy-five per cent earned by way of the completion of an assortment of assignments and tasks will pass the course even if they do not try and score or perhaps more properly "earn" a zero on the final exam. Obviously, apply some factor less than twenty per cent and the day-to-day course average could be proportionately less than seventy-five per cent.

What might be the justification for a final exam? Is the overriding purpose to determine how much students do retain and know overall after all? Why?

Through small segment periodic tests and perhaps other methods of evaluation, student proficiencies can be demonstrated and perhaps quite accurately.

What more might be needed? Then, is the final exam presumably required only out of lack of incentive or because of unwillingness to give up a tradition?

Perhaps the notion has not been given consideration.

Used differently, could the final exam have value in determining the effectiveness of teaching?

The competence of the teacher could be reflected as a final exam outcome. However, best student performance would have to be assured for the reliability of that assessment.

How could that be guaranteed? What could be the inspiration?

The motivating force could be to substitute the final exam score for the student accumulated score if it were an improvement. For some perhaps, that would be an incentive.

If not for all, would the sincere student effort be discernable from among others? Could a trustworthy foundation be established? Why persist if the final exam would be disputable in ascertaining teacher ability?

While rationale for the use of final exams is elusive, its continued use appears to be inescapable.

Consequently, why not make the final exam mandatory, a requirement for course completion, an information tool a survey of accomplishment.

Though why bother if it will have no impact upon the final grade?

Again, if the score were an improvement and applied as the final grade over that already accumulated, what would be the incentive to be responsible during the course if the "go for broke" option existed at the end?

Sincerity of student effort would be questionable under any

circumstance. Students would have the right of choice, an option at hand. Maybe that would be acceptable.

While of uncertain usefulness, of undetermined worth, the final exam, the believed to be all important tool of discernment, is undoubtedly a fixture in the classroom repertoire.

Then, if here to stay by tradition or custom, fittingly, what should be the content of the final exam, five, ten, twenty or even twenty-five per cent of what, of each topic presuming equal worth and significance represented by the so-called power standards? Or, should the final exam test in depth only those parts of the course that are considered most significant by designer preference or other mandates? What in the selection of questions insures final exam integrity?

Whatever that may be, it should be identified, forthright, and justified.

For the less than comprehensive final examination that was given to those students handed a so-called "practice final exam," no test and measurements data had been offered and likely no data was available that could show at least the congruity of each exam item with a particular target concept, objective, goal, or standard as it may be. Likely, no test item analysis measures were available for the individual items and the final exam as a whole.

Should this be a matter of need to know?

In matters of final exams, reliability and validity need to be established as well as the discrimination power coupled with the difficulty of each item. A count of each option should be done separated into categories of upper half and bottom half scores.

Given these analysis requirements, an assortment of other questions can be asked.

Could better test questions have been written? How would it be known? Why were specific questions selected for the final exam rather than perhaps several others? And, is any of the extraneous language use a problem for the test taker? Do the test takers know all of the pertinent vocabulary? How can that be established and test items perfected to do their job unless these and other questions are asked and due diligence is rendered?

One question on a department prepared final exam required students to have knowledge of the magnetic field of the earth. Though students that I had worked with were given the opportunity from a videotape to learn about the magnetic field of the earth, they responded poorly to the question.

Other students with another teacher did better.

Why?

That teacher was the test author.

Was it how the question was presented? Did this age group of students have the mental processing wherewithal to adjust, the flexibility of discernment to interpret the words of the question?

Of all that can be proposed, the first need that must be addressed is why "this" or why not "that" question? Then, are the students taught with a certain package of material able to grasp some or many of the thought to be highly regarded concepts taught using a different assembly? Are they mentally ready to make these adjustments seemingly dependent upon extensions into the realm of the abstract domain? Has sufficient time been taken to find out, to figure this out so that the job of education gets done correctly, presenting appropriate material appropriately leading to the defined place with the student ability clearly in mind? Does anybody know?

Some teachers flirt with criticism by offering take home final exams. Their desire to be comprehensive in discerning student learning leaves them vulnerable because no matter how demanding, the outcomes are questionable. As should be obvious, student workmanship always begs for authentication.

In reality, the employment of a final exam is how a major component of education does get done, maybe as much as twenty per cent. Regrettably, almost every facet of that can be challenged for its purposefulness at any given grade level except for very early on where learning the basics is undeniable.

The chicanery linked with the comprehensive final examination has no place in the classroom.

A story is told of a veteran social science professor being berated for having used the same final exam every year since he had begun teaching. His Dean said, "Don't you realize that students have been sharing your tests for decades and that all of your students know exactly what's on the exam before they take it."

The professor responded, "It doesn't matter. I keep changing the answers."

Doing what is right may take hours. Settling for less is to fall short. Integrity in evaluation must be at the bottom line.

Indeed the number of questions about learning and teaching as well as education in general is by far greater than the answers that can be provided.

How is it that students can earn grade point averages that exceed the top value of the range?

One small town newspaper article proclaimed the achievement of two outstanding students. One had earned a G.P.A. of 4.644 and another had posted a G.P.A. of 4.596 on a scale of zero to 4.0.

Indisputably, these graduates are intelligent.

But, how is it that their G.P.A is beyond the upper limits of the range? How can that be achieved?

Of course, the scale is weighted.

Ah, but how is the weight established and who decides the weight? For universal fairness, do other schools and agencies have or use the same bag of weights? If one course is weighted more than another, what makes one course more weight worthy than another? How much more worthy? Why?

Who can deny that grading is arbitrary taking into account all of its many facets? Compensation for the variances maybe the reputation attributed to an institution, school, or teacher. A 3.5 G.P.A. at school "A" may be held in higher regard than the same G.P.A. at school "B."

What is being "said" by that? Is it likely that at some institutions performance is consistently above the rest? Why do some try to set more "rigor" into place? Does this kind of grade scale waywardness have some purpose? Do schools participate in these posturing and muscle flexing shenanigans so as to appear "tougher" or "higher quality" or "a cut above" but in effect are disillusioned? Because of apparent successfulness embellishing a few, is it then that some may be proportionately disadvantaged? Is grade enhancement on the one hand a kind of injustice at least for some students?

It does seem clear that the intent of such schools is to lay claim to some kind of superiority position such as, "We are better than the school down the block or around the corner or our graduates are comparatively above the rest. We are a tough school with high standards."

Others as well may fall for the gimmick thus viewing the school as "high caliber." This is arguable, of course.

At least at one high school, the structure for toughness actually resulted in the creation of at least three schools in one whereby some students were in "basic" level classes with some progressing in the "regular" track and others in the "honors" grouping. Those in the "regular" level with some latitude were allowed the flexibility to mix in some "basic" level courses but were not permitted to take any courses in the "honors" level. The "honors" level could mix and match among all of the levels but were not expected to enroll in any of the "basic" level courses. Within this structure, the school actually had become a conglomeration of top-down countless possibilities.

How is all of this sorted out for graduation? Do the "honor" students wear red cords, the "regular" don white, and the "basic" get attired in blue? What if a student took courses from two groups? Do these students wear some kind of blend perhaps pink or purple?

Ridiculous as it is, what are the implications of the "conglomerate" system? Can that kind of situation get sorted out by others especially employers or college and university admissions officers? Will some students get a break while others are set aside? How might a college or university, transfer accepting school, or potential employer know who is who?

Did the student with a 4.644 earn all grades in the presumed 5.0

"honors" track or did that student earn only some "A" grades in that group with at least a few in the "regular" category classes? How would anybody know except to carefully analyze a transcript and know the particulars and specifics of each course? Is that expecting too much?

In mathematics, formulas often rely upon constants to achieve some kind of equalization among terms.

Why would a system impose a demanding "figure it out" requirement? Why inflict this burden? Alone, would reputation be good enough?

After an excuse or two, to alleviate the complexity, the school likely labels each course according to its rank, "honors," "regular," and "basic." In addition, the school could provide a rubric or even a catalog of course descriptions.

Who might care enough to decipher the criteria or who would care enough to overcome the inconvenience?

Regardless, realize that evaluation grids and descriptions too may be scrutinized differently with different sets of eyes.

Ultimately, the convolution becomes more or less like competitive diving wherein some dives are deemed more difficult than others for which the reward is greater of course only if the dive is performed as well as another dive with a lower rating. Thus, performing a highly rated dive poorly could earn the same score as a lower rated dive done well. Well, maybe.

The diver's score is accordingly adjusted and reflected in the total number of points accumulated by several judges simultaneously observing the dive. So, classes viewed as higher level, likely more demanding, get more arbitrary "base-line" points for the grades that are achieved. That does make sense, perhaps. But, that may not work in offices of hiring officials and in college or university admission offices without multiple observers with scores or grades averaged according to some conclusive predetermined classification.

As an alternative, some businesses associated with food, travel, and entertainment use status ratings that reflect the available facilities. Similarly, transcripts of academic accomplishment could be garnished with "stars" typical of hotel, restaurant, or movie ratings. For example, the student earned a B+ grade in a 3 ½ star course.

What does that say? The problem is still the problem. What constitutes a 3 ½ star course? What combined set of elements determines a 3 ½ star course?

On the other hand, what if a system is set up as in gymnastics where up front, the difficulty is established by what authorities have declared more or less difficult; for example, a vault of 6.6 points compared with 6.5. Deductions are marked off from a ten point standard score and then added to the difficulty value. A competitor now can never earn a "ten," what was once a "perfect" score.

An inclination might be to say, "Does it matter? Enough! Get over it. Even if schools were to somehow standardize grading and decide to buy into the application of the same criteria, guarantees cannot be made that grading outcomes will be different, universal and reliable."

Nonetheless, if a student in the "regular" level track earned an "A" grade in every class the maximum achievable G.P.A. only would be a 3.0. The justification might be, "The student still could enjoy a 'feel good' mind-set." Maybe that would be a consolation.

But, how fair is it? What can a "D" grade average in "basic" level courses earn, only a G.P.A. of 1.0 or less?

All of this can become confusing and it may be extrapolated to include at least a little if not a lot of arbitrariness. The concern is over whether or not employers or admissions officers can make sense of this kind of grade maneuvering and manipulating.

Admittedly, in some states by mandate, students of lesser ability are accepted into the state university only because they rank in the top ten per cent of their graduating class. Other students in highly competitive schools who have higher success probabilities are set aside only because of this kind of compensation.

Obviously, "good" and "bad" as well as controversy can be found in everything.

The university that I had attended as an undergraduate operated with a 4.0 G.P.A. scale but an "A" grade was ninety-three per cent or above; the lowest "B" grade was eighty-five per cent; the lowest "C" grade, a seventy-seven per cent; with the lowest "D" grade set at seventy per cent.

Comparing my grades with an equally demanding university down the block so to say, my G.P.A. looks pale. But, please note that I earned a lot of eighty per cent scores that were awarded only 2 G.P.A. points compared to 3 G.P.A. points at the other university. My meager 2.46 G.P.A. may have been as good as a 3.11 at the other school. In graduate school, with a more conventional grading system, my G.P.A. was a 3.79, not spectacular but agreeably better than 2.46.

Who would know? Should anybody care? What is reasonable? What is right?

A three point something G.P.A. for whatever reason always looks better than a two point something G.P.A. for any other reason.

The bottom line is that these non conventional systems invariably disguise and/or distort reality.

Did the student with the 4.644 G.P.A. actually earn a grade average greater than "A?" Did this student achieve at 116 per cent compared with others who earned an "A" on a 4.0 G.P.A. scale? Does anyone know? How would anyone know?

The tangle remains.

How is anyone assured that students with their earned or assigned G.P.A.'s are evaluated and subsequently ranked according to students from another school or school system competing for limited places in the job market or for the limited places of the incoming freshman class at a choice college or university?

Nobody knows.

For the sake of evenhandedness, it would be helpful if schools agreed to and then adopted some common rating system.

Perhaps schools should adopt a four point ranking system with each point having some conventional value and then stick to it. In that way, those who sit at graduation would have some assurance that the student with the distorted 4.644 G.P.A. is really equivalent to a more universal 3.644 G.P.A. and deserves to be the valedictorian and is among the brightest students graduating even compared with other students in other schools.

What then would determine the reputation of a school? What reliable alternative qualities would have to be put forward to set one school apart from another? Would that be necessary? What would determine a "blue ribbon" school?

On the other hand perhaps national rating competitions should be employed founded on generally approved criteria determined by some national panel of experts. Perhaps regional, state, and national academic "quiz game playoffs" could determine rank order. But, we just went through that with final exams.

Is that putting evaluation into the hands of another? Is that standardization in another form? Or, is this a lot of "to-do" about nothing?

Truly, G.P.A. determined and calculated by whatever method has little to do with the status of a school or the abilities of a student.

Rather it is somehow decided arbitrarily by generalized opinion of the supposed behavior and quality of its graduates, mainly their performance in the marketplace.

As a result, please let us stop trying to create an artificial advantage or inadvertently a false barrier for the students trying to go on in school. Give up on artificial loftiness, trying to impress the competition or anyone else.

What can be counted on is that deviously or otherwise at least some schools will tend to inflate themselves to create an image. It is a "lizard brain" thing. Perhaps, it is somehow set in place by natural law.

15

Some universities consider themselves as "good" or possibly "great" when they raise the bar.

The main campus of one state university will not accept a student unless that student is in the top twenty per cent of their high school graduating class even though the average of state placement test scores for the graduating population of that particular high school is in the top two per cent of the state.

A student in the top twenty one per cent of that high school is still within the top two per cent of all the students in the state. That is way up there but unacceptable.

Would some agree that this university is shortsighted by a policy that in all likelihood grew out of an uppity or more likely an out of touch disposition? Why the top twenty per cent? What is so magical about that? Is it likely that this university appears to be shooting itself in its own foot with its failure to meet the needs of many quite able students?

Of course, these students are never turned away. They are invited to enroll in many other universities nearby and across the country. By almost every university, every student or at least most of them graduating from this particular high school should be welcomed.

With such a shortcoming, how is it that this state institution of higher education is held in esteem?

Its purpose should be in providing learning opportunities for every interested person.

Is something incoherent with an admission criterion that prohibits the admission of high performing students who attended a notable high school? And, where are the people to object?

However, in countering this admission requirement, the high school no longer ranks its students. Oh, the loopholes in qualification generate the foundations for deception, all must agree.

Years ago, through a National Science Foundation grant, I attended a summer institute on radiation biophysics. Certainly, one of the professors was brilliant maybe without comparison. He had earned several advanced degrees and at times the language of his presentations was beyond the scope of the participants. At these moments an older teacher would nudge me and say, "That's why higher education doesn't get any higher."

Is this remark on target for at least selective colleges and universities? Are arbitrary restrictive and limiting admission policies another reason why higher education does not get any higher?

Another public university will not accept students unless they have earned an essential curriculum diploma. Likely, these students would have been enrolled in the "regular" or "honors" tracks wearing the red or white academic paraphernalia at graduation.

Is this policy another example of thoughtlessness or even selfishness?

Reasonably, if aspiring higher education students are screened before they have a chance to perform, they may never have an opportunity to perform at their best.

While leading a science and mathematics department meeting during the time of my employment at a small college, the president barged in furious over the lackluster performance of nursing students on the National League of Nursing test (now replaced by another certifying examination). Many of the students had failed miserably.

It was the contention of the dean of nursing that the instructor of anatomy and physiology was at fault. The president indicted her with teacher irresponsibility and demanded that she abandon what he considered to be a "crème puff" take-home final exam. His tirade was relentless. He insisted that the students be given instead a rigorous and demanding final. He spent considerable time providing justification for his request.

The next day, as the storm subsided, I had requested a meeting with the president to discuss his concerns in more detail. I needed to know how the people of the nursing school came to put the blame for failure squarely on the anatomy and physiology faculty member. In the pursuit of that interest, I was given permission to search through the nursing student records including course grades and admission test scores.

To the chagrin of the president and the dean of nursing, a correlation analysis of the data strongly implied that the NLN test results were directly associated with scores on college admission tests. The coefficient of correlation was a convincing 0.71.

Without hesitation, the ultimate consequence of this study was to raise the baseline score on the admission test from thirteen to sixteen. While still considered marginal for success in college let alone nursing, at this higher cut-off point, the correlation study predicted correctly that over ninety-five per cent of the graduates would succeed on the NLN test. And, they did.

Unfortunately, the outcome of the study was contrary to my most earnest feelings. The results led to the wrong outcome. My work confirmed to the leadership that to achieve high performance scores, the focus should be upon up-front "weeding and sorting" rather than upon teaching that makes a difference.

Can it be defended that the nobler course of action should have been to help candidates who might be less likely to succeed by introducing alternative teaching programs that might enhance their all around skills?

As is typical, rather than search to see what could be done to uplift students, the matter was resolved by raising the bar. Apparently, the same holds true for our high school and even elementary school dispositions.

Reasonably and basically, higher education has a twofold purpose. First and most important of these is the obligation of transmitting the heritage whereby all can benefit and second, as it can, it should contribute to extending the frontier of knowledge.

If correct about my assumptions the following two examples are contrary to current policies in higher education.

While in industry, I did meet a young man who was absolutely brilliant in machining parts. He had a unique ability to visualize the finished parts in the raw materials, certainly not unlike Michelangelo who undoubtedly visualized the Pieta in the block of marble before he had chiseled it into its final form.

One day while on the job, I made an attempt at encouraging this young man to continue his education to perhaps earn a degree in mechanical engineering.

He replied, "Been there. Done that."

I asked, "What are you telling me? I do not understand."

He answered, "I already tried that. Some time ago, I went to sign up for some classes at the 'last minute' community college down the road. But, after talking with the admission's officer, I would be required to start with Introduction to Algebra. That's arithmetic. I explained that I wanted to begin with geometry, that I already knew all the algebra I wanted to know and that if I realized I needed some additional algebra, I would sign up for a specific course at that time."

As might be expected, the admission's officer refused to accept his plan. In essence, this young man was told, "Like it or not, this is the policy. We do not allow exceptions."

An ill advised functionary faithfully following a set of arbitrary pre-requisite guidelines made a determining decision affecting a lifetime and future.

As a consequence of the encountered rigidity, will anyone ever know if this young man would have succeeded in his academic aspirations? Emphatically, how dare anyone limit the potential of another? Is that the way higher education should make itself available to interested clientele? Who are these perhaps too many misguided people that represent the purposes of higher education?

Actually, at public institutions, every course on the menu should be available to anyone with the money to pay the tuition and the willingness to try if, of course, seats are available. Certainly, those enrolled in prescribed degree programs perhaps should have allotted preference.

That is not outrageous as some might think. It is the only way.

Every post secondary adult person or those in high school with the "right stuff" should have access to higher education at whatever entry level they choose. Without regard for prerequisites that might be nobly imposed to assure success, all should be welcomed. The opportunity for success should be rightfully theirs. As everyone should be afforded the right to succeed, equally, everyone should have the opportunity to fail.

Everyone seeking education should be held accountable for paying the required fees for the courses of choice as well as working within the framework of the syllabus while maintaining a positive and productive disposition that does not infringe on the wholesomeness of the classroom environment and that does not limit the timely progress of the course.

Schools were not made to be barriers. They should be for everyone vehicles leading to new opportunity.

About the time that this young man was struggling with his frustrated ambitions, an adjunct faculty member from this same local community college came to my office to discuss the possibility of some in-house computer technology training. As we progressed in our dialog considering needs and services, he arrogantly commented, "Well, today is a day of reckoning."

I responded, "How's that?"

Rather arrogantly he said, "Today I'll be giving final exams. I'll be separating the wheat from the chaff."

Without hesitation, this wannabe professor was told, "That is outrageous. It is wrong of you to think that way. How can you call yourself a teacher? As that is your point of view, to 'weed and to sort,' then we cannot use your services here today, tomorrow, or any day after that. We at this company are about enrichment and enhancement, the development of people into all that they can be without settling for less."

In another situation, a dear young lady severely hearing impaired from the antibiotic treatment of a childhood illness went off to school hoping to earn a degree in nursing. Enthusiastically and optimistically, she had signed up for all of the prescribed first semester classes.

To the dismay of this academically naïve young lady, on the first day in General Chemistry I, the brash professor boldly announced, "I urge you all to look around this lecture hall. Today, you see well over 250 that have gathered here. Do not make too many friends because after the first test, less than one half of you will remain. And, by the end of the course, scarcely fewer than one hundred will be here."

Seemingly, this professor was intent upon driving students out rather than upon the more noble cause of making available to them the provisions to excel.

Needless to say, the heart of this aspiring young lady was crushed. She thought, "How could anybody be so cruel?"

Little wonder why higher education does not get any higher.

Strength of personal character would have to prevail over the disappointing behavior of those more than should have to be tolerated misfits that represent higher education.

After class that evening, the young lady with tears in her eyes called home to announce that she was going to drop out of the program. Of course, her parents were dismayed. Be assured that within a few days, the vice president for instruction of that university offering an apology sat in the home of the young lady. However, the would-be nurse by then had chosen an alternative path through another university that appeared to offer a gentle and more accommodating environment.

Against great odds, this young lady would eventually earn a Master of Science degree from a highly regarded university. This noble university including its professors understood the most significant part of their mission: teach well those who are yours to teach.

Today, the young lady is helping others manage as they navigate through the distress of their particular circumstances.

While it is important that college and university professors are curious, education in general would be better off if they instead were focused upon improving their teaching especially in transmitting their sought after knowledge.

Research is a specialty of a few uniquely gifted. A human failing is the tendency to redirect interest and energy. In general, individuals tend to do something other than what they signed on to do. So, teachers, teach well especially the up and coming teachers of the next generation. Be devoted to that great cause.

16

Within seems to be a driving inclination to improve, to make everything better. Recognizably students are asked or required to measure up to higher and higher demands. More, more, and still more is added, more pages to cover and more work from upper levels shifted downward. Little consideration is given to the needed knowledge, skill, and true intellectual prerequisites. This could be one of the major problems facing education, getting it right. It is quite possible that what is taught in schools is thoughtlessly expanding beyond reasonable limits.

But, are schools and their constructs the only culprits?

As may be commonly known, a Clarence Darrow aspiring apprentice tried repeatedly to pass the bar exam but over and over again, failed. After each unsuccessful attempt, he would return to the office with shoulders slumped with disappointment written upon his face. However, one day, his effort paid off. He was notified that he had passed the exam. He was ecstatic. The next morning upon entering the office, the young man exuberantly shouted alerting everyone that he had succeeded passing the bar exam.

On hearing the news, Mr. Darrow slowly raised his eyes from his work and said, "Forget not your torments. When some day you are given the opportunity to write the test questions, make them more difficult than those that were imposed upon you. That way those in the future who struggle with the test will hold you in admiration, a testimony of your accomplishment."

Should this young man garner more admiration than he had earned?

Are teachers victims of this same disillusionment? Are accomplished representatives of society expecting more than should be expected? Do they puff themselves up making learning more tedious and difficult for the next generation? Do they expect others by age less mature to accomplish in hours what may have taken days or even years for them to achieve? How can they justify themselves?

Would they likely say, “You know it’s about success, maintaining our place, the economy? We have to stay ahead of the competition.”

But, it is for someone else having to carry the burden, the next generation.

Similarly, textbooks have become a part of the burgeoning problem contributing perhaps significantly in raising the academic bar. In the mid 1960’s a typical general biology textbook contained 792 pages. It weighed just slightly over three pounds. A current general biology textbook has grown to 1138 pages and weighs only a shade less than six pounds. In pages, this represents a forty-four per cent increase in forty years, approximately two generations.

True for one textbook for one course in one subject area, is this proportional across the curriculum?

No doubt other examples could be sited. Then multiply this increase by five different courses.

What is expected of today’s student? Is it really appropriate? Can a claim be justified that textbook expansion is at least a contributor to the shortfall of United States students compared with others in the international marketplace? Can thoughtfulness prevail or is that asking too much?

The addition of pages represents one kind of problem but the included content represents still another more formidable quandary, the abstract concepts that students are required to grasp.

Do they have the wherewithal? Why did our students fall behind? Could it be because what is expected has become too wearisome? Would less lead to an improvement if it were judiciously sorted out from the available mass?

What happens to those who cannot reach the academic bar? What happens to those individuals who are personally fragile, those who lose heart struggling to reach the bar just out of their grasp? Do these likely become disheartened and disenchanted? Do they fail? Do they give up and eventually quit? Do their scores drag down the national average? What happens to them? Do these students become those left behind?

Through the best of intentions, the curiosity in learning and the motivation to learn seems to have been destroyed maybe not in all students but likely those that have to work hard in learning.

What options does a young person have?

While some might withdraw quietly, others subconsciously realizing they are left behind may grow to resist and fight back. These are likely to be the detractors and distracters within the teaching-learning enterprise.

Could there be a relationship between some classroom behavior and academic demand? Has anyone attempted to make a connection to figure this out? Might less actually be better?

It may well be a consequence of the intense competition among noble hopeful textbook publishers, to be more attractive to selection committees with each edition containing more pictures, figures, and charts. Teacher editions also include the support of huge amounts of margin information and notes: teaching tips on presentation, "factoids" and tidbits of all kinds, as well as answers to questions. All in all with merit.

However, the increasing glitz for at least eye appeal and more growing content for the involved and ready to go teacher even at the expense of reasonable and appropriate does not guarantee a sale. What used to be the attractions, booklets with teacher guidelines, laboratory and workbook activities, and test question banks are essentially ho-hum.

The new lures include an array of gimmicks: a day-to-day word-for-word teacher to class presentation series and electronic planner.

Yes, some textbooks come with a daily script for the presentation of each lesson. It is impressive beyond words. A word-for-word presentation is available for each day. Just read it to the class. It goes something like this: "Recall, yesterday we covered "dah. dah. dah." Next, remember we went over "la . . . dee . . . dah" and so on. Of course, this feature is intended for the new and inexperienced teacher who just could be overwhelmed with learning the ropes of teaching, those to skip and those to jump.

As well, the planners are special. Teachers need only to plug into the program the adopted school calendar of holidays, classroom minutes, recess periods as well as the start and end date of the academic year. In the blink of an eye, a day-to-day schedule will be provided that will optimize the presentation of course materials. The teacher will be given a set of daily lesson plans of what to do Monday through Friday throughout the school year whether 175 days, 180 days, or even 200 days. Every moment of classroom time is allocated. Every test day is set. Every page will be covered ready or not. Wow!

So, if all of this is available to the seasoned or newcomer teacher, what is the need for a teacher anyway?

Have a functionary come into the classroom and read the notes, provide the materials, and execute the plan. Teacher creativity and imagination that bring about unique and individualized wholesome experiences essentially have been set aside for uniformity and obviously academic collapse.

If the non teacher in the classroom were viewed as reasonable, who then would have to shoulder the blame when outcomes are less than desirable, the textbook publishers?

However, the big plum that turns eyes to saucers tempting textbook adoption committees is free stuff, lots of it, in the amount of about ten to twenty per cent of the cost of the books. Not bad or is it?

The foremost question should be what about the book even with the tossed in sweetening of laboratory equipment or classroom materials? Is it worth it?

Upon independent review, a book packaged with all of the relishes had been adopted though it had been seen as thinly written, so succinct, so synoptic, and so scant in presentation that it had been considered too emaciated to be generally understandable. It was thought that students after reading it would be hard pressed to build concepts. Nonetheless, the plan had to be executed. Adopt the book. Get the equipment. Shelve the new books and use the older more readable textbooks from the previous adoption.

Why?

The answer was simple. The equipment was wanted and needed to replace the old worn out thingamajigs as well as some homemade gadgets, "junk" from generations ago.

Again, why?

The answer was not extraordinary. The budget as it had been set up would not allow for the purchase of replacement equipment. It had available money but fixed in the wrong places. Essentially, the budget had significance only because it was given that status but it did lack the integrity and trust necessary for it to work flexibly and favorably.

Purposeful teachers will get what is needed though through deviousness. Certainly, they deserve credit for their crafty thinking, their manipulative workmanship, and their overall resourcefulness to set up labs with equipment that will help students learn.

School systems could do better. They could trust those whom they hired to do whatever is needed to get done what ought to be done in the right way.

However, why are the budget keepers so unyielding? Is it a matter of control?

It does not appear to be about doing what is right.

If teachers who make up the adoption committees were trusted, their equipment recommendations would be honored. Then, the outcome would be what is appropriate with the movement of money to the correct budget lines that would enable the purchase of essential replacement equipment that would then enable a judicious adoption of the most suitable books that support proper classroom instruction.

This method does make sense. It is logical. It is not in any way underhanded. It is the correct thing to do.

Then, why are administrative systems so convoluted and administrative agents so covetous of their position?

Anyway, should teachers be the ones writing textbooks? Should publishers respond to the needs of teachers rather than impose their own all exclusive efforts?

That might lead to some kind of bedlam. That would be risky. But, what emerges might be better than could be imagined.

John XXIII once said, “Open the windows. Let the fresh air in.”

Could that thought be translated into the world of academia? What then?

Diversity in line with the dictates of nature might be honored.

17

If considered necessary, the development of state standards ought to be a job that depends only upon the input of very thoughtful individuals who first have a clear image of the people they look to graduate. They should be based upon a thorough needs assessment rather than fabricated from the personal interests and biases of their composers. When written, they should be clear in their intent and meaning. Unfortunately, the standards as they are written require interpretation that is itself arbitrary.

As my father-in-law describes food, "All is good. Some is just better than others." Standards should be above and beyond that.

Every standard and element within should be comprehensively scrutinized for its specific contribution to the development of marketplace-ready Good Citizens of Earth. Given the global condition, society cannot afford anything less.

While noble and worthy in some contexts, the standards need to measure up to the definitive test, the ultimate question, "Does the standard in every aspect correspond with what will be required of every person?" Should everyone have to master every standard?

If yes, then all standards as written must have inherent and universal merit. Justification needs to be provided.

Is the standard clearly interpretable? What are its specific contributions? How does measuring up to the standard, teaching it and learning its elements, add to the formation of globally able individuals?

The following two standards can be evaluated for their contribution to both of the established criteria. The first is taken from an environmental science list. The second is for a course in general biology.

> *Know and describe how ecosystems can be reasonably stable over hundreds or thousands of years. Consider as an example the ecosystem of the Great Plains prior to the advent of the horse in Native American Plains societies, from then until the advent of agriculture, and well into the present.*
>
> *Explain that some structures in the modern eukaryotic cell developed from early prokaryotes, such as mitochondria, and in plants, chloroplasts.*

The first standard, powerful and thought provoking as it seems, is apparently designed to lead to the understanding that natural resources as those represented by the grasslands of the Great Plains need to be protected from deterioration not unlike other areas of the world as the Amazon rain forest, Asian Step, or everglades and even the oceans including fish species and coral reefs.

However, the advent of the horse is likely insignificant in its impact. The horse, few in relative number when introduced by the Spanish, would have been a competitor of the bison that roamed in the abundance of the grassland. On the other hand, the plow, not mentioned that might be implied at best, was the significant intruder affecting the condition of the Great Plains. Once secured by settlements, the great grasslands were under the indiscriminate and more so ignorant control of its new occupants who at first out of the will to survive focused upon the cultivation of farms.

In accomplishing this standard, the students need to understand the totality of noble earth citizenship. Into this concept, they can develop the readiness to analyze the problems associated with the thoughtless and aggressive use of not obvious but limited resources.

As was the case with the Great Plains and now with the Amazon Forest and the everglades, the earth just cannot be torn up with disregard. The belief that the systems of the earth are indestructible is nonsense. As it ought to have been in the past, students, to be decision maker occupants, need to see and understand this standard in the context of the big picture, the global situation. Students should be led to understand the need for earth compatible lifestyles. They need to be directed to understand the need to build strong international economies where no one is left behind. They need to be shown that greed must be set aside for the common good everywhere in the world.

The first standard as it is written should lead to the worthy achievement of a lifestyle mindset that is compatible with worldwide ecosystems rather than focus on the arrival of the horse and the not so competitive impact that it may have had on the grassland.

It would require days of interactive classroom instruction. It would have to be thoroughly sorted out, broken down into several defined objectives that then could be individually treated, quantified, and tested. An array of questions would be needed to establish its overall accomplishment making the grade in all of its various aspects, exemplary or proficient, and then in particular whether students had achieved some measure of application.

Why make the standard so comprehensive and open for interpretation? Would any teacher be able to get it right? Would sufficient time be available to cover every dimension? What should be kept? With deference, what should be set aside? Why? Does anybody know?

The second example while also well intended is only theoretical and has relatively little impact on the development of essential concepts of biology other than for those who may be keenly interested in evolution at the cellular level likely not a high school student.

How did these state standards come about, one that is overwhelming and the other rather superfluous? What could have been their inspiration?

Who decided what should be included and listed under the heading of standards? Who crossed the “t’s” and dotted the “i’s?”

What were the criteria for selection? How were these derived? Could other standards have been written? Were they written after the content of textbooks? If so, should it be the other way around? Should input be gathered from a greater range of resources?

Are the standards to be the end all for the efforts in teaching and education? What gives confidence that in teaching to this set of standards rather than any other set, students are better for it? What gives credibility to the notion that with standards, students will catch up academically with the rest of the world leaving none behind? Again, does anybody know?

Note that each course is represented by perhaps forty-five standards. With a school year of maybe 180 days, fewer than four days can be given to the accomplishment of any one standard.

If all standards are to be covered, which are to be stressed and which are to be moderated? Again, why?

Presumably, state standards are determined by committee in response to a perceived need to enhance and to enrich the knowledge base of the present and following generations. For this direction in education, commonly the marketplace leaders are sought out, the professionals; attorneys and physicians; businessmen, chief executive officers and small business owners; and others such as clergymen and representatives of non-profit organizations.

The standard writers represent a significant resource that at best can provide a point of view, profile, or silhouette of sorts. Beyond that the standards need to be handed over to be further developed considering the elements that are workable in the classroom.

A lot of professionals need to be on board to complete this really important part of the refinement process. The range might include elementary teachers through college and university professors.

However, some recent reporting suggests that higher education appears to need at least as much help as does the secondary schools.

Nevertheless, given the complete range of academic professionals could something fitting and reasonable get configured?

The questions may include, "What is the route from where students are to where students truly need to be? What are the specific or absolute bottom line elements that must be included? What should be the bare bones of accomplishment and how might it be ascertained? What should be expected beyond the minimums? What latitudes should be available that allow for individuality and permit going beyond the limits? Is it reasonable that extra credits might be awarded? How might that be accounted for?

With due regard, why not demand as much of the colleges and universities? Certainly, who would be bold enough?

But, would an effort in improvement result in increased demands for secondary students not unlike the high school teacher asking for more from those in elementary school?

It seems that every teacher wants every student more prepared for their next level of learning even to the point of becoming prohibitive unaware as they are and well meaning as they may be.

Clearly, the job gets done in the classroom. The nitty-gritty of how the jobs of teaching and learning really get done belong to the teachers and students. From the onset, these two often set aside groups, elementary and secondary school teachers should have been factored into the prescriptive process. The reasonable conclusion, "Those most needed are the most overlooked."

As recognized, for teaching to be appropriate and on target, the starting point has to be identified by way of a thorough needs assessment and the end point must be clear before a route can be properly devised. These provisions will insure desired achievement that does not have to be to establish place in comparison with others but rather and most importantly that all accomplishment is first and foremost for its own sake.

For better or for worse, the standards did come about and undoubtedly, as they are, here to stay. Nothing that is added to the bureaucratic system resists removal more than its own inertia no matter how urgent the cause may be. Simply, standards as they have come to be inevitably must be dealt with after the fact.

As such, should the standards be utilized more as a set of guidelines rather than a fixed list of this is what everyone needs to know as if somebody really does know? Should the standards be relegated to the principles of a set of essential core values?

Core values make up the cornerstone for the most successful enterprises. Not recognized in education, they are more than the often posted mission statements. They establish identity. Core values emerge from the very heart of purpose, the fundamental ideology of the institution.

Then, should these core values have been identified first even before a needs assessment? Should those core values as determined singularly direct the thrust of teaching and consummate learning?

With a set of core values in place coupled with a reliable needs assessment, the standards would have had to undergo thorough scrutiny if education were patterned after the style of business. Still, the question remains whether or not standards do improve education or whether they are appropriate or do they increase the obsession for answers thereby limiting the scope and range of learning.

Certainly, the application of standards in industry did improve the quality of manufacturing and if the plan to continuously improve on every detail were implemented, the system of education would surely improve not by quantity but by quality, the most important aspect of all.

On the other hand, should other less specific goals be encouraged such as individual innovation, creativity, curiosity, and inquiry that lead to problem solving? Would it be too bold to teach for the attainment of abstract not so readily measurable goals? If this were done, could teachers be held accountable? How could their effort be measured?

The plan for accountability as it is known would dissolve. The approach would have to be changed. Clearly, these more abstract intangible goals or preferably ideals would be outside of the basic criterion objective domain.

Would the next generation be better for expanding the scope? Are those involved reluctant to take a chance, to conduct the experiment? Perhaps schools should be commissioned to implement and evaluate different approaches gleaning out what works best rather than follow a universal prescription of questionable merit? Is what is good and working in New York City equally as good and workable in Los Angeles?

Everyone in education is expected to give wholehearted unwavering support for the established standards and see to it that every student is so enhanced unless the creation of academic waves can be tolerated, unless turbulence in life can be accepted. Appreciate fully that school systems will be scrutinized and teachers will be evaluated with endowments held as leverage.

Who would be willing to stand apart and face the perils of impending no doubt arbitrary assessment and criticism if otherwise success could not be established by objective testing? Who is willing to put their job on the line? Is anyone out there?

Going back to my high school days, I recall a wonderful and informative chemistry class taught by a teacher new to the school system. He was inspiring. Students looked forward to his class. He taught to assure learning and taught all that could be managed in a classroom. But, at the end of the school year, when the students were taking the citywide test (the school system might be considered progressive considering this occurred during the mid 1950's), I noticed that this teacher, as probably others new to the system, was copying the questions onto a pad of yellow paper. Not unusual for the time. Copy machines were not yet available. Documented objectives were not yet applied.

Was my high school chemistry teacher proclaiming something profound? Was he attempting to sidestep the purpose of those then considered benchmarks for learning now called standards?

No doubt about it, the next chemistry class that was taught by this teacher was on target with those criteria. My chemistry teacher was not a fool. Certainly, this teacher recognized that his future employment and salary as now in some school districts is at least in part dependent upon student performance measured by the school system standard based examinations.

Could the utilization of standards be driving education in the wrong direction?

As they may be well intending, they may be creating a kind of circumvention not unlike the book adoption that secures needed laboratory equipment. The classrooms may become purposefully focused on answer getting and test focused teaching and little more.

Should teaching be more than that, more exhilarating and inspiring? Should it focus on enrichment and enhancement rather than upon the limited and confined, on the journey rather than the destination?

Sure, those who manage to climb to the summit are remembered but the journey is most memorable for those who try.

Several related questions still remain given that standards however derived, in a steady state or not, are the route to follow in education.

Why is it that all courses require the same number of days and minutes for completion? What is so magical about a 180 day school year or a ninety-day semester or a class period of fifty-five minutes?

It does seem reasonable that some subject areas would require more time for completion than others.

Would it be outrageous for one course to need only twenty-nine days while another ninety-eight days?

Noticeably, the present system of education is not unlike the young lady cooking ham. The way it is, everything fits into the box and everything that lasts ninety days gets its predestined state assigned single credit that fits accounting more than the needs of essential increments of learning. If more time is allotted than needed, pack in some extra could do without elements. And, if more time is needed than allotted, the course of study will be overloaded and students perhaps overwhelmed with cannot do without essentials.

Given this rigidity, the classes, students, teachers, as well as the academic day and even school year are scheduled.

Is the proverbial tail again wagging the dog?

In industry, the watch words are, "Think out of the box." In contrast, in education, everything as such needs to be put into the box. And, one size fits all.

Will this thinking end? When in education will the stuff in the box get emptied out and carefully examined for its merits and true worth and given an appropriate priority place?

Licensure especially in school systems is a serious restriction upon talent though it may not appear as such. Justifications may be provided and arguments can be presented, many very capable and highly qualified people are denied the job of principal or even teacher only because of licensure. They are typically locked out of any opportunity. Motivated by recent necessity praiseworthy pathways have emerged that enable access of military veterans and an assortment of retired business professionals.

Fortunate as I see it, I had been able to start teaching and begin a career in education without having a license only because at that time a private school had a bit more latitude.

For what it may be worth, I wonder, if not a teacher, in what career might I have ended up?

While uncertified, working both in the fulfillment of academic degrees and licensure requirements as well as teaching in the classroom, I had earned quite a few favorable comments from administrators, colleagues, and students and I had been encouraged mostly by students at all levels to continue. The foundation was intuitiveness, nothing taught to me by a licensing provider.

So, does licensure make the person? Does licensure provide assurances and security that capable people are in charge?

Not really.

An administrator's license can be achieved with something in the order of thirty to forty graduate credits. The training concentration is upon leadership, counseling, history, philosophy, and psychology coupled with at a few universities an apprenticeship period that may be the most worthwhile of the requirements. Having some form of firsthand exposure, individuals can work with the everyday problems of an administrator as the job is. Yet, as important as these tasks are seen to be they are not what the principal ought to be doing.

The job of principal should be all about education: overseeing the totality of teaching and learning. However, none of the courses have to do with the management of education or with developing master teacher skills certainly the priority.

So, does a license really certify a "good" administrator or for that matter a "good" teacher?

As it may need to be, the day-to-day management of a school easily could be partitioned to several others all based in a central office presuming a school community is composed of more than one campus site. Each would have precisely the required wherewithal: behavior control expertise, business know-how, and building and facilities supervision. Because personnel would not be duplicated, this arrangement might even cut school operation costs.

During one after school moment, I went out of the building to be in touch with an Assistant Principal. Buses were in rows, several teachers were marshaled to stand in the parking lot, police officers were nearby, and most surprisingly, the principal was shouting to students to board their bus so that they could be on their way, this day, in two minutes. Incredible but this was done every day.

Is this what a high school principal should be doing? Does it have anything to do with licensure, being good at your job, or overseeing the necessary functions of education?

At another school, I recall the principal being out in the middle of the street leading to and from the student parking lot. He was dressed with a crossing guard vest. In hand was a stop sign to direct traffic so that students could safely leave the premises during a snowstorm.

Agreed the actions of this principal were noble. Looking out for the safety of the students may indeed be one of the priorities of the position but should it be the concern of the principal at all? Should that responsibility be in the job description of the principal?

Does the principal directing traffic make sense? Should the principal have delegated the priority? Could someone other than the principal have done this? Should the principal have been working on other matters of educational significance? What would you have the principal do during the work of every day even if in the midst of a snowstorm and even during those other exceptional days?

And, what should be the duties of teachers?

While sitting through a three day workshop on the discernment of standards, I met a young teacher who had recently graduated from a prominent state university.

I inquired, "How do you feel about what you are doing here? Are you learning anything that you do not know already?"

"No. This is all new to me," she replied.

I continued, "Then, what did you study when in the university?"

She answered, "Oh, I guess the usual. After the two years of general studies courses, I completed courses in my major area, and then went on to do the education courses."

"What was that all about, the education that is?" I asked.

"Hmm, some education history, theory, methods, and practice teaching," she said.

I continued, "And, what did you learn in methods?"

"Mostly, writing lesson plans," she answered.

Surprised, I asked, "Lesson plans? No data analysis or tests and measurements?"

"No, not really," she answered.

I replied, "How then can you be held accountable in teaching if you are not in command of the tools by which you will be at least somehow measured?"

Our dialog was interrupted by the presentation of a new workshop segment that featured "Father Guido Sarducci on the Five Minute University" by comedian Don Novello.

At the time, I contemplated, "How true is this, 'The Five Minute University?' Is that the outcome of all education? Will students say something similar to that about my classes?"

All present did laugh no doubt because at least in part the videotape was a more or less accurate satirical appraisal of what is retained with the completion of a four year academic degree. Maybe that is all a bachelor's degree can offer. If true, this provides further argument for the restructuring of schools.

Should a teacher be better prepared or differently prepared?

In addition to subject area expertise and ideally tests and measurements competence, should a teacher have more in their professional repertoire? Should teachers have a mental framework that inspires interest and motivates learning? Should teachers have a positive outlook disposition founded upon a concept of individual importance?

How much hope can a teacher inspire? How much concern should a teacher offer?

Overall, teachers are caregivers who must offer trustworthiness to each and every student and encourage unrestrained curiosity.

19

Of late, accrediting agencies have added school wide improvement projects to their list of evaluation criteria. These projects are intended to focus on some particular and possibly unique area of academic concern.

As I have found, the responsibility is fixed upon the principal who as I had experienced lacked the means to effectively handle the task at hand. While well intending, the accrediting agency had imposed upon the principal a circumstance that was certainly outside the range of his capability in statistical measures as well as positive interactions with faculty and staff.

Of course, the solution was to offer up a workshop or two on how to deal with the added obligation. Consequently, the principal would have to slot into an already overburdened calendar a couple of days for growth and development. Likely, the outcome would be good but the capability should have been in place long before.

For example, because of marginal student performance or because of some ambition, a school or school system would be expected by the accrediting agency to work on the improvement of performance in a single aspect of growth and development. The effort might focus on an element of a statewide basic skills assessment, a tool devised to determine school success by way of student achievement at various grade levels in various areas such as reading, writing, and arithmetic.

As I had discovered, the objective and logic of the principal was clear: improve scores on one or two of the specialized test areas and total scores will go up. With that determination, the appropriate questions ought to have been, “What specific areas need to be improved and how can or how should this be accomplished?”

That was not how the project unfolded.

As the principal had attended, I was asked to be present at a similar workshop but the presenter did not deal with anything related to how a project might be set up and put into place with an eye on the specific measurement of outcomes. Rather, the workshop provided by the accrediting agency focused upon the most basic statistical parameters, mean, median, and mode.

While sitting in the workshop meeting considering the simplicity of the data parameters, several schools proposed to set up projects for improvement that were likely outside the scope of quantification.

The teachers present did not get it.

The representatives of one school proposed, "The Improvement of Student Interrelationships" no doubt to have a "happy" school.

While projects of this kind have great merit in their intentions they need to be adjusted so that improvements can be more than just faculty and student testimonials. Perhaps the completion of appraisal forms would be acceptable. Though not considered, tallies could be gathered from students and faculty then tabulated to get some hard numbers into the various categories of the bell shaped population distribution curve.

Apart from the workshop, the principal who no doubt huddled with a select few confidants put together "to-do" lists that were subsequently given to the balance of those on the faculty as if mere functionaries who manufactured isolated parts that eventually would be assembled into a practicable whole. At this point, the system fell short, again.

Certainly, a multitude of options may have been available, a multitude of issues could have been considered. The process would have been tedious and would have required patience. However, all of this had been overlooked perhaps for the sake of some urgency perhaps nothing more than, "Let's get this over with!"

Ideally, in the first place, a diverse panel of individuals should have been called together to work collaboratively to suggest specific improvements that truly would have made a difference in the performance of all students. Then, once identified, the specific objectives and means could have been defined and mechanisms for achievement could have been designed, configured, and developed; sensible and congruent evaluation mechanisms could have been outlined, evaluated, and put into place. Again, this could have been done collaboratively. This was beyond the thinking of the principal.

Everything needed for the study could have been uncovered by way of a school wide effort consistent with prerequisite fundamental questions. At each of the various grade levels, students as well could have been included in the project set-up. They might have been able to feel some partnership having been included.

In dealing with identifiable elements, what kind of improvement would be acceptable? What level of achievement would be acceptable? What evaluation instrument documentation and analyses would be required to assure reasonable confidence?

Certainly, "brain-storming" would have been the reasonable place to start but out of conditioning would everyone be listening and contributing or would the interests of a single individual namely the principal prevail as had occurred?

From my point of view, the first action must always be mutually shared. Get everyone involved. Achieve buy-in. The worthwhile outcome would be all in agreement or when all is at least agreeable.

Consideration is a priority. It must be demonstrated if teachers, students, and possibly staff members are to become meaningfully engaged and involved. Then the expectations of each participating individual or group can be defined and made clear.

Questions that always need to be addressed include: Are all courses amenable to the selected project? What protocols are needed? What steps and intermediate steps will be used to lead to the acquisition of intended outcomes whether they are knowledge structured or skill based? Why were these criteria established instead of possible alternatives? Should a list be limited? How convincing is the justification for any of the listed options? Are any more or less absolute? Why? What measures are applicable? Are the main objectives and their subsets substantive or will they provide for only "make you feel good" results?

The list of pertinent questions can go on and on. Reasonably, all need to be considered.

The school project that had been selected was to improve student math test scores on the state mandated student assessment in the area of data analysis covering frequency tallies and interpretation of data represented in two graphic forms, Stem and Leaf plots as well as Box and Whisker diagrams.

Although this may appear to be a solid project that would render quantifiable data, the across the school program had several inherent defects. Not all students take the state test in a given year, only a few related questions were included on the state test, and the outcomes of the state tests could never be analyzed to determine if the effort of the project produced any improvement concerning those items. Only the total score would be documented. The test would certainly vary from year to year and teachers come and go.

Internally, the project would fall short because not all subject areas could equally respond. For example, an English class commonly does not deal with Stem and Leaf plots or with Box and Whisker diagrams for that matter. In house test questions would have to be analyzed for congruence and test item analysis would have to be included as a part of the project from the beginning. This was never done.

All of the interacting elements of any school wide improvement project should be considered at the onset and the project should be designed and developed under the tightest of possible constraints for it to have significance and merit. Mostly, it was the expeditious, make it up as we go program.

Results on in house tests were quantified as above and below passing but none of the needed tests and measurements elements were applied to determine overall effectiveness of the project.

Really, what is the purpose of these accrediting agency imposed actions? Are they intended to give assistance to schools and students that lag behind or are they more likely a means that will be used to impose accountability of sorts and assign failure as may be needed or perhaps even award blue ribbons? Are they by design pushing schools to look into their processes and methods with an eye on improvement?

Ironic as it may be, because schools are in the business of knowledge transmission, the presumption is made that they are learning organizations. That is not the way they work in practice. Quite by accident, accrediting agencies may be bringing this about by demanding of schools the implementation of improvement projects.

In all, the role of each and every individual in education, student, administrator, staff member, and teacher, needs to become different than it is. They need to become self-reflective and assist each other in a continuous process of perfection although perfection may be out of reach. It is about trying to be better in what is yours to do.

20

Years ago while serving as a science department chairperson, I was given the responsibility to head up an Instructional Resources Committee. It was composed of eleven people including a student as well as myself. This was viewed as a token committee that would placate an accrediting agency requirement that the faculty were an active source of input into the administration of the college. It had been set up to oversee the activities of the library especially the media center. No one expected that a meaningful outcome would materialize. Never before had one resulted.

Before a first formal meeting, I visited individually with each committee member. I met with them in their respective offices to describe what I hoped the committee might accomplish. I saw instructional resources as a lot more than tending to the demands of audio and video taped materials and projection equipment. For me, instructional resources included the faculty and students as well.

Acting on this footing, each faculty member and the student representative had been asked to prepare a list of several most important matters that could be pursued by the committee. They were asked to complete the task within a week. Also, I asked each if it would be acceptable to come by their office to pick up their list that would be compiled with others and then distributed for review by all. Without hesitation, it had been agreed. When the compiled list was distributed, each had been asked to select the three most important items and mark them in order of importance. They were asked to have this completed prior to the first meeting scheduled one week later.

Surprisingly, three items surfaced as most important including faculty development, student retention, and finding common ground. It was agreed that one matter should be considered each year. Faculty development was chosen as the first most significant matter of concern. Until that time, it was haphazard if any occurred at all. The other matters were to be studied with recommendations to the administration over the following two academic years.

Subsequently, the issue of faculty development was divided into subcategories with two and three individuals taking on the responsibility to research each subcategory according to their interests and strengths. The next meeting dealing with reports on findings was scheduled for one month later.

What is important here is that each individual was involved. The work of each was valued. And, a timetable for task completion was established and precisely followed. The follow up was important assuring completion. Especially early on following task assignment, each member was personally contacted and encouraged about their role and the importance of their contribution.

After the subcategory reports were given to the committee, the members were asked to study the information and develop a plan that would lead to a program for faculty development. Within the context of the following meetings, one month apart, the outline of a proposal was achieved: drafted, approved, and submitted to the administration.

The process here is important more so than the actual plan that was developed. It follows the guidelines of empowering management essential in the articulate operation of business and industry.

Needless to say, the college administration reviewed the proposal and put into place the committee recommendations that included a monetary award if an application for faculty development were submitted and approved, meaning within the framework of the college mission statement. One accepted stipulation was that all of the allocated money had to be dedicated and totally used each academic year for individual faculty or college wide programs.

Outcomes hinged upon mutually wholesome and respectful interpersonal relations. Collaboration was the spirit. Selfishness for any reason as might be associated with top down management had been prohibited. Convincing arguments had no place within the structure of a panel in search of solutions. They were essentially outlawed. An authentic feeling of openness prevailed among the members. None were privileged and none assumed the entitlement for responsibility. All affected entities, faculty members including the student, were involved at the onset and throughout.

Thoughtful feedback mechanisms considered essential were established at the beginning to insure input of every kind so that information, data, and proposals could be gathered and assembled into an agreeable and workable plan of action. This was strategic planning in action and it applies equally to the design, implementation, and evaluation of instruction.

Consideration must be given to how teachers, students, and possibly staff members become meaningfully engaged and involved. The expectations of each participating individual must be clear. With a collaborative working relationship as a foundation, a learning organization can be established. It is odd that schools in essence are learning organizations but only in concept. Little of what a learning organization is happens in schools, that is having a determined focus on continuous self-improvement.

The learning organization concept began to emerge and permeate business and industry in the early to mid 1990's. Certainly, it is the outgrowth of the quality control measures that now are widespread throughout the global market including the management of telemarketing though this may seem a little odd.

How is quality control applied to a telephone call?

However, it is in place as a means of monitoring professionalism, word usage, and interactive time in making sales. It leads to the discovery of "how to's" and "what for's" in any business. It leads to the development of best practices founded upon lessons learned. More of this is needed in education, in schools, in helping the next generation to learn. This may lead to a truer form of accountability.

The businesses that foster a learning organization atmosphere emphasize a variety of imperatives: learning based upon experienced consequences; learning that seeks to put into place the procedures, methods, and techniques assuring positive gains; and learning that results from proactive initiatives, being aware of what matters most, setting aside the likelihood of negative outcomes. In addition, interpersonal relations learning is essential that includes personal mastery and shared vision dispositions.

All of the learning that proceeds needs to be set into an organizational context that includes a vision for growth and development as well as a strategy for achievement. Both a culture of productivity and structure of performance are essential if not critical. This can only come from solid well formed generally purposeful leadership.

The guidelines of learning organizations are directly applicable to schools that need to function as does any enterprise according to quality control dictates monitoring their success and productivity in line with the principles of throughout the organization development.

21

Considering that growth curves are exponential, could it be that learning curves are exponential as well? What would be the outcomes of different students starting at different levels? What impact would this have on the ending level of achievement?

It can be expected that the individual starting at a higher level potentially will more quickly end up at an exponentially higher level. Consequently, merit pay as implemented by some school systems should be based upon not where individuals end up but rather on the difference between where they might be expected to end up and where they actually do end up.

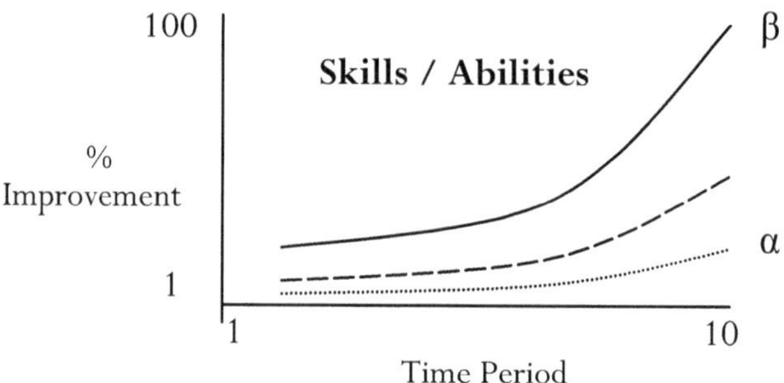

For example, the student, Alpha, in the level three group of his class may start out at the one per cent position of attainment ability. This student persists in learning skill "1" through time period ten. From the growth curve, this student may be expected to show a threefold improvement or acquire skill improvement to the three per cent mark. On the other hand, the student, Beta, beginning at twenty-five per cent position of attainment during the same time period might be expected to improve to the seventy-five per cent level.

The improvement by both Alpha and Beta would be threefold.

However, the end score of Beta would be seventy-two per cent better. Alpha improved by only two per cent while Beta improved by a notable fifty per cent as expected and shown by the chart. If teacher "X" directed the improvement, the teacher performance certainly would be considered more than acceptable. Both students achieved at their expected levels though Beta did score a lot higher.

If the student performance outcomes were an identical threefold with Alpha having been taught by teacher "X" and Beta by teacher "Y," who would deserve the merit pay?

On the other hand, if Alpha improved to five per cent with teacher "M" and if Beta improved to eighty per cent under the supervision of teacher "N," who should be applauded, "M" or "N?"

Which of the two teachers brought about the greater outcome? On the other hand, what if Beta improved to seventy per cent instead of seventy-five per cent?

It is likely that the teacher of student, Beta, will always be more highly regarded just because the final score is higher. Likely, any award would be based upon the highest percentage of attainment rather than upon the ratio of improvement.

Which is more important, gain or end point? Who is the one deserving of recognition the one who mediates the greatest change or the one that accomplishes what could be expected?

Based on history in education, achieving the summit seems to be more important than the journey. This appears to be counter-productive if the mission of the school is to raise students to recognized new heights.

By connecting teacher pay with student success could schools be rewarding for the wrong reasons because learning assessments may not take into consideration the beginning point or potential? Should teachers be assessed by the change they may bring about on a probable projection curve?

In one state that recently adopted a merit pay system, teacher effectiveness as represented by student performance will determine an increment of pay increase.

For example, teacher "D" has five scheduled classes each has a mix of students some exhibiting "off and on stress syndrome" and others just blatant "refusers." Only a few students try to work to their fullest. In general, the majority of students have a history of failure. However, teacher "D" works long hours in preparation and provides excellent presentations but in the classroom everyday he struggles with behavior issues.

Will teacher "D" be able to earn any merit increase?

On the other hand, teacher "G" has five delightful classes with only a few students exhibiting learning barriers. Overall the students have a history of high performance.

At the end of the school year, final exams measuring the achievement on standard tests are given to the classes of each teacher. The average score of the students of teacher "D," is sixty-six per cent. Based on previous performance, their scores averaged at sixty-one per cent. In contrast, eighty-seven per cent is the average score for the students of teacher "G." Their previous performance average is eighty-two per cent. The scores of both teachers went up.

Which teacher should earn the merit pay increase?

Based on record alone, is teacher "G" the most likely recipient because the per cent score was greater and comparatively the final scores were twenty-one percentage points higher than for teacher "D." However, teacher "D" did a truly outstanding job in attitude adjustment but has little to show for it. The small gain demonstrated by the students was enormous considering their starting point but the intangibles provided by teacher "D" cannot be quantified.

Considering the day-after-day effort, teacher "D" had a positive impact on the attitudes and dispositions on many of the students but not all. Some students lived with tremendous difficulties and shouldered perhaps overwhelming problems. More than expected, the students did at least try to do a better job if only just a bit.

I know firsthand because I have been there. I do know what it is like to believe at the end of the day that you have accomplished nothing yet perhaps may have made a difference for a few. I do know what it is feels like to have worked as hard as anyone could work but come up feeling short in production.

Merit pay is not the answer to the problems that face education. One teacher will be elated while several others will scoff. The reward for one is not worth the risk of disenchantment for others.

The problem is in how education is done and perhaps assessed. For the most part, teachers teach and schools function maybe as established by tradition. They do what they do because that is what they have always done not unlike the young woman cooking ham for Thanksgiving. This could be depressing except that the solution may be in rethinking the methods, in restructuring the system.

What should be the entering data for any proposed essential skill? What instrument can be used to determine its baseline? Are any of these values known? Which of all the student skills and abilities should be of greatest concern? Consequently, how is it possible to link salary increases with teacher performance when the essentials are beyond the operational database?

Some projections have been made that suggest eighty percent of the students can master the material of high school, not just pass with marginal grades but actually master the material. Along the way, many of these students have been sorted out by their early on pace as well as by the feelings and emotions of teachers that they encountered. In the beginning learning stages, they may have needed more time to develop the mental constructs essential for grasping the critical concepts. They may have needed some one-on-one support but could not be accommodated if possibly justifiable and likely not so understandable reasons.

From papers and articles about stroke survivors, mental processing is not unlike a house with many shut, open, and yet-to-be opened windows. Some stroke survivors have been found unable to communicate in their native or early childhood language but can converse in a language learned later in life perhaps through travel or during college studies.

That is rather interesting. It implies that language learned at different times in development seats itself in different parts of the brain. It correlates well with observations that suggest that children have more facility in learning languages than do teenagers or adults. Obviously, the "seating" of language at different ages occurs differently and in different parts of the brain. Thus, at an early age, the window for language development in one part of the brain is open and facilitates this type of learning. Later, that window closes. Then, language must be accommodated through an alternative window and "imbeds" differently albeit with more difficulty.

Perhaps spelling skills and facility in vocabulary are most accommodated early in life by a special window then later with this window closed alternative seating arrangements must be made again likely with more difficulty.

Is it this way with other abilities, perhaps with mathematics and science requiring at least some abstract thinking ability?

Early school programs appear to support this notion. If true, then setting a youngster aside in deference for an arbitrary have to cover the material premise is unjustifiable and must be considered intolerable.

How can accommodation be offered to every student in every class?

When in the midst of work leading to a master's degree, by teleconference, I met Dr. Samuel N. Postlethwait. He described a teaching innovation, Audio-Tutorial Instruction. The approach developed from a resolution to accommodate students who missed lectures. Rather than repeatedly review his presentation for each inquiring student, he began the audiotape recording of each class and then left the recorded tape in the library for access any time by any student. As time passed, the lecture hall became increasingly empty. Instead of attending lecture sessions the students went to the library to privately listen to the presentation. He began supplementing the audiotapes with demonstration items, visuals, and specimens.

Over time he thought, "Rather than have the students go to the library, why not offer them an alternative by placing several tapes with support items in a laboratory room staffed with an assistant who could if necessary answer questions that students might have as they progressed.

Truly, individualized instruction had its humble beginning but with the application of current technology, so much more can be made available to the students that will personalize learning that will enable them to learn efficiently and effectively, more in less time.

My doctoral research was all about individualized instruction. However, my spin was to account for the significance of each element in the instructional sequence to the point where if "that" were desired then "this" must be done to get there. In addition, business management tools were uniquely applied in the analysis of specific instructional systems. In effect, this is the only way educators can discover the value and purposefulness of various strategies in the process of teaching that leads to learning.

Assuming teacher credibility and know-how, individualized instruction coupled with systems analysis methods is the cornerstone of real accountability. Not the accountability that is submissive and surrendered to an outside authority but an accountability that enables teachers to firsthand find out for themselves, as they should, what is working in getting the results that are needed for their students.

Furthermore, the methods of individualized instruction enable teachers to be more creative within their responsibilities because they do not have to be in the continuous presence of students for learning to take place. Assistant teachers and tutors can accomplish this quite well. Specific results can be observed and evaluated for every implemented element. Lesson fine tuning is possible. Teaching can explode into excitement with curiosity at its base.

Individualized instruction thoughtfully implemented has the capacity to maximize opportunities for most of the students most of the time when coupled with guided discovery strategies. Today more than at any other time, it can take advantage of the enormous range of computer technologies. Individualized instruction assures that every participant endowed with special and unique qualities will be able to fully take part in learning though quietly and inauspiciously.

However, be assured that a teacher needs to be available when students encounter difficulty or when they seek insights and a broader perspective. A guideline may be, though struggling but succeeding leave the student to their task. Only intervene when they are failing in their endeavor. This is a lesson learned from General Dwight Eisenhower as he described a parenting approach obviously quite applicable in education.

In addition, individualized instruction gives students the opportunity to have learning flexibility. They can come and go without losing their place. They can recover from mental lapses without having to rely on someone else for secondhand information. They can focus and concentrate without distractions. They can go backward and forward through a lesson tying together all of the elements. Individualized instruction is a great vehicle for both teaching and learning. Expect that students will be able to accomplish significantly more with perhaps improved scores.

22

Where I had grown up as a child and teenager, under the philosophical influence of William A. Wirt, several schools were constructed to have a south facing main entrance.

Apparently, before my day as a high school student, it may have been considered at least one of the significant factors. Reasons were never given. It was just that way. But, prior to my freshman year, a building addition had been completed. The entrance was changed to face the east.

As a teacher, I had wondered, "Did the change result in some altered impact on learning, an impairment of sorts? Does it really matter from which direction students would enter the building? Is the direction of entrance a determinant for the making of a good school?

Is a good school one that is built so that sunlight shines upon the entrance illuminating the front of the building throughout the day? Does sunlight add to its quality, enhance learning? Does the metaphysical outcome of sunlight upon a classroom window have anything to do with learning? Could other elements be as important or more significant? If yes, what might those be? What are the substantive ingredients that go into the make-up of a good and worthy school?

Most teachers as I have observed with sunlight exposure keep the blinds closed. Amazing! In some way could this be suppressing quality education? Nonetheless, how depressing. The vitamin D that might be synthesized is needed for a brightened outlook that might even lead to a more favorable reception of teaching. Upon inquiry, the response is, "With the blinds closed the students cannot look outside. They cannot be distracted."

Why might the students be inclined to look out of the window?

Likely it is out of boredom because of what is going on inside the classroom causing most students at least subconsciously to plead with the gods, "Let it be that I may be some other place out of here."

The question remains, "Is a good school determined by the configuration of the buildings and campus, the equipment and facilities, the programs and extracurricular opportunities, the administration and teachers? Which of these is foremost among these parameters? Which is the most absolute determinant?

From news reporting, it is obvious that athletics get more attention than poetry reading, art display, music recital, or theatre presentation, even the science and mathematics fair. Why?

Is it again a matter of interests, "brawn over intellect?" Is it a "lizard brain" tendency that leans toward competition, a fundamental construct of survival? What if a school supports its athletic program with first class playing fields and indoor equipment? Is a school better because of its programs of engagement?

Athletics does play a meaningful role in developing student wholesomeness. No doubt about it. In addition, parents and other members of the community can rally in support of their children as well as those of neighbors and friends. Spirit can be conveyed. Cheerleaders emerge to promote unity and support. The importance of teamwork can be taught and simultaneously learned. A common identity with all of its ramifications can be established and secured, the joy of success and accomplishment coupled with the pain of shortfalls in performance. Some aspects of personal identity and true worth can be impartially defined. The values of family and community can be transferred, distributed, and shared.

With all of its added value, with all of its countless contributions, with all of the enrichment that can be derived, schools generally have achieved most of their lasting substantive recognition because of intangible qualities associated with those accomplishments that are outcomes of study and learning linked to marketplace professions.

Are at least some inclined to agree with that assessment?

Surely, athletics and athletic facilities valued as they are cannot determine whether a school is good. Other more lasting meaningful elements have to be a part of the totality such as the facilities and the contributions of an assortment of individuals that support an array of general and specialized academic programs.

What is a good balance and mix that maximizes the opportunities of each student in school?

As much glitz as can be pointed out and as many physical structures can be leaned upon, facilities alone are not the answer in the creation of a school or a school system that exceptionally provides for all of the students enabling extraordinary progress.

If it is reasonable that physical structures do not determine either quality or worthiness of a school then should budgets be aligned with what is significant with what does determine the excellence of a school? If it can be asserted that facilities do not determine the merits of a school, could it be other ingredients, the students, teachers, and administration? Is it some one entity or combination of components that can be found emerging from within the community, trustees or even the staff members?

Clearly, I recall walking to school each day through a beautiful park abundant with trees, shrubs, and flowering plants; boasting a pavilion and band shell; and spotted with wonderful recreational facilities. It was a special place. It was a special setting for a good school. Little more could be desired.

Who would not want to attend that school? Who would not want to teach at that school? Who would not want to be responsible for its outcomes?

Without a doubt, good schools are born in the midst of good communities. With some rare exceptions, the people are the foundation for the development and accomplishments of every good school. Collectively, the correct vision, proper motivation, and persistent determination are what communities contribute giving the cornerstone for what emerges.

The community in which I lived my early years did not have a lot of money but it had a lot of wealth derived from personal integrity coupled with future mindedness and the dreams that were kept for its children. From these reserved, humble and hard working steel town people would emerge the social configurations, the staff that supported the school, and the trustees that gave the school its positive and fulfilling direction. Unquestionably, it is a translated attitude that determines the context of real and lasting wealth. However, out of some undetermined convention, the inclination is to look to the one given the authority as well as the responsibility for action, the principal.

Are the principal and the associates at the top of the hierarchy actually the determinants of whether a school is good or not? Clearly what is the role of the principal and others of the administration?

Be assured that in most schools, principals and those in proximity with that office more often than not are occupied with a multiplicity of overwhelming issues not at all related to the emergence or maintenance of a good school. Their preoccupation is with public relations and resolving social interaction problems, building and landmark construction, facilities management, budgeting, and assignment scheduling rather than the mechanisms of teaching and learning. If the list were prioritized in order of importance, seemingly image and its relatives are significantly more urgent than core values, mission, purpose, and outcomes.

This can be confirmed with a time study. How are the moments of every day allocated among the various responsibilities?

On a wager, the most important of all responsibilities is the most neglected. Sure the principal starts early in the morning and works late into the night focused on doing a good job. Perhaps this is an exception but in a little over two years all supervised by the principal, a new gymnasium/classroom complex had been constructed, a several acre athletic complex was in the making, annual fund raising auctions were held, countless reports to trustees and accrediting agencies were filed, countless discipline policies were enforced but obviously, none were in direct support of learning, the primary purpose of a school.

Obviously, these functions that could be well done by others have little or nothing to do with education. In the day-to-day routine, little time is devoted to leading the development of teaching and the progress of learning. It is taken for granted that teachers in place do the job. Most of the time is set aside for accommodating the demands of various influential or controlling agencies requiring work on only superficial academic improvements.

As I returned to the classroom, I was impressed with the amount of teacher independence. The school seemed more like a shopping mall with the principal serving as its general building manager and with teachers operating in classrooms not unlike shopkeepers doing business. Presumably, if at the end of every day, the facilities were intact and the students were reasonably mannered, a good job had been done by all. That seemed more important than whether the students were properly engaged in learning strategies leading to significant concept development.

How would my supervisors know? None showed a sincere interest. None visited except to fulfill the annual observation requirement. They were too busy with their assortment of tasks essentially not related to either teaching or learning.

Early on in the profession, I met a well adapted business teacher who had in his desk drawer two as needed lesson plans that were devised for any impromptu administrative or supervisory visit. He was pleased with this deviousness insuring that he would never be caught off guard.

Today, this situation is not likely to confront a teacher. Again as experienced, classroom visits would be set up in advance with ample time provided so that teaching at its best could be observed. Before the observation, teachers would be invited to submit their lesson plan that would absolutely correspond to a goal in the curriculum guide that would match up with some mandated state standard.

As an outcome of some thoughtfulness, it has become my contention, that the principal of a school should be more like the head football coach of a National Football League team. Whether the stadium is clean and tidy are not his concerns. If the concessions are truly refreshing and tasty are not among his worries. Likewise, he is not likely to be interested in the parking facilities or the network of transportation that brings spectators to games. On the contrary, his obsession is only with the quality of the team and the performance of each player. Presumably, he is talented above all in his assignment and is supported in his effort with several assistants and assistants for the assistants. These are in place to insure that all of the work is carefully planned and the plan is meticulously carried out.

If the analogy is acceptable, then as it is, the job of the principal is upside down. The principal is on his/her head in their assignment and needs to be turned to stand on his/her feet to be right side up to respond appropriately to the level of their responsibilities. The concept of the principal as it is should then be replaced with the vision of a master teacher assigned with the singular responsibility of teacher success and student performance. The singular function of this master teacher would be to move individuals to their highest level of workmanship. If the master teacher position were established in a school, everything about the school would suddenly change and would open up countless new possibilities for advancement.

First of all, the commonly expected duties of the principal would be reassigned to an assortment of personnel. For example, the duties of image could be given over to a public relations expert. Fund raising could be delegated to an outside marketing agency. A chief financial officer could deal exclusively with budgets and the education focused prioritized distribution of funds as needed. Student behavior could be managed by guidance personnel.

Experienced support staff could handle reports and the details of relevant research. Someone might even be assigned to deal with the issues of the cafeteria, vending machines, and parking lot.

The mall like school would be transformed into what it was intended to be, an interactive school. It would be a school having an environment focused entirely on the interconnected simultaneously occurring teaching activities including each and every classroom each and every nook and cranny of the building and its landscape. Everything that relates to learning would be intricately coordinated.

Working to orchestrate the learning enterprise of a school, the master teacher would enlist the contributions of highly qualified associate teachers, one representing each significant academic area: language; art; music; humanities; social, economic, and political studies; mathematics; science; and technology.

This group with the aid of assistant teachers would develop the curriculum to meet the needs of purposefully educated Good Citizens of Earth. Collectively and collaboratively utilizing the forces derived from a division of labor, they would design the methods of instructional presentation with built in accountability systems for the analysis of every detail. Enabling this, instructional packages would be predicated upon well defined and predetermined goals and needs assessment based objectives, all of this resting upon a well articulated mission statement derived from representative core values.

Presumably, if the instructional systems achieved the desired outcomes, they could be used as models for designing instruction that measured up to other similar learning needs. If the instructional systems were to fall short, those identified areas of weakness could be modified and adjusted until the intended results were achieved. This kind of system enables continuous tinkering leading to steady improvement of instructional methods. It is the foundation leading to the thoughtful development of instructional theory. It is the only true system for accountability, internal self-accountability that matters and motivates honest success.

When this concept of restructuring the school staff was presented to a friend, his reaction was, "What you are suggesting would require many more teachers. How would you pay for this?"

Actually, if teachers could do the kinds of work that they should be doing, each would contribute in the support of a differentiated staff. But, this arrangement might actually reduce the number of accomplished professionals and even reduce the academic overhead. Certainly, it would enable students to have more direct contact with frontline teachers and other assistant personnel. Perhaps through this contact, more students would learn more and more students would grow in the possession of contributing dispositions emerging as the needed Good Citizens of Earth.

Maybe society would need fewer jails with the resultant reduction in operating expense offsetting any additional financial burdens if any taken on by the schools. If each teacher each year would be able to influence the thinking or mindset leading just one student to a productive life that might not otherwise take place, over the lifetime of the teacher in the classroom this would add up countless dollars that could be classified as truly beneficial to a community and society as a whole. At a social cost of $50,000 per year per inmate, the offset should be obvious. It is better to have teaching staffs that have a positive impact than to have overburdened faculty and administrations that manage at best each day to get the work done as prescribed by necessity.

Einstein once said, "Insanity is doing what you have always done expecting different results."

Perhaps it is time to realign the structure of the schools to work for truly positive outcomes that support a wholesome society filled with anticipation coupled with the enjoyment of prosperity.

23

Now, who would argue that the bottom line for the success of any school rests in the combined capabilities of its human resources: invested community, managers of education and associated teaching professionals coupled with the interactive support of assistants and apprentices in an individualized instruction format?

Assistant teachers with their apprentices in the classrooms in collaboration with the work of the associate teachers and the master teacher ultimately responsible for the totality of teaching and consequent learning would be able to present thoughtfully designed instructional systems in conjunction with student support materials. With this arrangement, instructional team building would be in place in a hierarchical structure that enables individual promotion and advancement within the teaching structure. As important, in this configuration, instructional development would be able to progress in a "kaizen" continuous improvement learning organization fashion.

Significantly, children in school especially in the early years would have the opportunity to seek help from more than one individual assigned to a classroom. It would prevent a single teacher from dominating children with whom a personality difference could reduce performance.

In this framework, teachers would no longer have to wait in line for their turn to get assigned to more desirable classes only after someone with more seniority on the job either retires or moves on to another opportunity. Real advancement from beginning teacher to master teacher would be possible based upon real accomplishment.

Currently, options do not exist for advancement except for moving up the pay scale with more credits, advanced degrees, or years of service. Really all that is available is some lateral move in the current structure into some more desirable environment seen as the chance to teach higher level courses perhaps with more learning amenable students or to move on to what may be perceived as a better school. For some teachers advancement is to work their way out of teaching into some higher level of responsibility such as curriculum director, assistant principal, or principal within the organization or to head up a more reputable school system.

This is not real advancement. It is a substitute, a perception.

Advancement is the opportunity to become better at what one is called to. It is to be recognized for the effort, the outcomes of study and research in teaching leading to the design of systems, strategies, and methods including implementation and evaluation techniques that promote efficient and effective learning. This kind of work truly substantiates true worth as a teaching professional not unlike the work of a researcher whose effort leads to the treatment and remedy for some menacing illness.

In addition to enabling the growth and development of both associate and assistant teachers, apprentice teachers would be present to enrich and hone their skills. They would be in an environment that directly would facilitate students assisting in small group configurations and in one-on-one tutorial situations and bring to the table their observations as well.

It does not get any better than this.

If learning is what is truly desired, this is the kind of ideal setting in which it likely would happen yielding recognizable gains. Student opportunities predictably would grow enormously. Enrichment, enhancement, and creativity could flourish and be appropriately rewarded. For very long, students would not be able to say, “I’m lost.” Always, someone would be available to resolve that need.

In addition, the burden for teaching teachers how to teach at least could be shared in conjunction with the domain of higher education or not at all.

Reasonably, can professors in higher education expect to be the teachers of teachers when many of them themselves struggle with the processes and procedures of teaching?

Years ago some state schools and colleges were in the specific business of teaching teachers. They were the experts in their profession. They were teachers in what were identified as normal schools and later teacher colleges. However, the lust for growth and development overtook their satisfaction with an apparently modest though special role in education. The result is not ideal especially in the preparation of secondary teachers.

Graduates of these schools may be well prepared in the theoretical and telling aspects of teaching propped up with technology supported slide presentations but they need more work in the "how to" of teaching especially in the preparation of laboratory materials and for student use instructional related aids. Today, the shortfall is compensated with supply house provided disposable kits for every conceivable laboratory or learning situation. Worksheets now make a difference commonly more than one for every textbook chapter. To some, this might be great but as a person cannot be proclaimed a chef using already prepared frozen dinners, a teacher cannot mature through the implementation of ready to serve canned laboratory investigations and classroom activities.

With everything done for them, how does teacher imagination grow? How is teaching curiosity maintained? More importantly, how are these qualities transmitted to the next generation?

Perhaps, higher education should just prepare future teachers with only the needed subject area background and the necessary theoretical tools. Essentially, higher education should provide just the general studies and liberal arts that can serve as a solid foundation.

In-training supervised teaching even by another name would be no longer needed. Should an individual choose to enter the teaching profession, the needed teaching and interactive skills would be acquired firsthand on the job. Many highly skilled and outstanding individuals would then be able to enter the teaching profession without having to deal with the commonly imposed burdens of state credentialing mandates.

Again, what really is certified by a state issued document, anything at all? Does having a license assure that a person is at least a marginally competent teacher if not a good teacher? What makes a good teacher, a license?

Licensure can certify only subject area competency. But, would a diploma do as much?

Are teachers born not made? What about the teaching profession? Is it an art, a craft, or combination of both?

Teachers as needed must be in command of the subject area for which they are responsible. Regardless of degrees, a teacher has to successfully demonstrate overall competence by some measure not skewed by source preferences. In addition, they should be secure in classroom management. They should be able to completely deal with their responsibilities, enrich ability and skill, and to improve on both directly in a classroom working side by side with proven teachers. Indeed, teachers should be able to earn the responsiveness of students.

First, teachers should be perceived as professionals doing a job that others might not choose to do or cannot do. Of course, if teachers do teach the way they have been taught then everyone and anyone should be qualified to be a teacher. On the contrary, if good teachers need to be prepared with certain definable masterful abilities and skills those qualifications will in effect set them apart from all others. This scenario suggests that teachers can be made but among them are those that have special intuitiveness. Perhaps these with inherent insights are those that are born to be teachers like no others.

Second, teachers always should be focused on their professional work. In some cases and maybe too many cases, they are distracted by "moonlighting jobs" whereby they may earn an extra dollar or two. A survey of sorts might resolve the issue but it appears that this represents the hallmark of "you get what you deserve and you deserve what you get."

Teaching deserves a definitely dedicated commitment. A general lack of incentives may be partially to blame but if the business of teaching is viewed only as a conduit, little more can be expected than a compromised performance. One cannot serve two masters.

The work of a teacher should be exclusive and involve the development of a common pool of knowledge that can be sorted into a prized collection of wherewithal with the potential for continuous improvement. Teachers need to find ways to superbly do their jobs and transmit this heritage to those who choose the profession.

Far beyond in the classroom learner management, teachers need to develop prowess in the configuration of teaching for learner development. Recall that the application of self-accountability programs are essential so that teachers can perfect the tools of their trade including the presentation of the most current subject area insights and the enrichment of presentation methods that enable students to learn with efficiency.

Years ago, self-accountability was an undisclosed norm. Teachers knew when they did their job well. They constantly looked for ways to improve even upon their accomplishments. Test and measurement statistics were available for data analysis. Forgotten, it is reappearing as a tool for school improvement but mostly confined to pre-test and post test result comparisons.

In one school system, all of the teachers are now required to participate in workshops intended to develop the most basic data analysis skills. Here we go again, back to the forgotten beginning, another example of the wheel being reinvented. Nonetheless, remarkable!

Teachers need to be prepared as guides in the process of discovery as the general heritage is conveyed. In this, they can establish a pattern, template, form, or construct for problem solving that is an essential real life marketplace tool. As is recognized, the marketplace needs more than a memory bank of knowledge. The marketplace requires the ability to make decisions and to appropriately deal with problems. The marketplace calls for gathering of information as well as its comprehension, analysis, evaluation, and synthesis.

Teachers need to be forthright with their students expecting mastery implying one hundred per cent competency or at least competency demonstrated at some prescribed level of performance such as get-it-right most of the time if not always. Why not!

Foremost, teachers need to be caring. They need to exhibit the adoption of wholesome and noteworthy personal core values that assure concern for the welfare of their students. They need to provide validation for the participating individual student. Fortified with self-discipline, mindfulness of others, and with empathy, they can expect the needed student receptiveness and eagerness.

Several years ago as a member of an international service organization, I heard a guest speaker describe some of his experiences as a judge presiding over juvenile criminal cases.

He said, "Before I sentence these young offenders, I make it a point to ask why they believe that they got into trouble in the first place. Surprisingly, almost all declared, 'Because my parents don't love me.'"

The judge continued, "Then I ask how they know that?"

According to the judge, these young offenders would consistently reply, "Because they [my parents] always let me do anything I want."

What might be some indicators of caring in the classroom?

In addition to being forthright, straight forward, and matter of fact with students not giving them the latitude to do whatever they want, teachers have to connect with them by being honestly interested in what is their interest.

Students are most responsive when asked about their goals and what matters most to them and when asked about what socially affects them in school and at home. Then, teachers have to empathize with students and be mindful of their concerns. The bottom line of this is that students recognize caring as a sincere concern for their progress and for their welfare.

Clearly, the preparation and development of teachers needs to follow a broader approach, a method that should extend beyond the limitations of licensure, that at best is the recognition of a minimum number of completed subject area credits.

Recognizably, a good school is more than a heap of bricks or stones stacked and arranged into some form facing a given direction for the reception of light. It is one that has the unique capacity of honing those most noble, compatible, and interactive qualities that characterize a complex and wholesome individual. The wherewithal is maximized in a learning organization environment ideally led by a master teacher with the support of associates, assistants, and apprentices working for the noteworthy interest of each student bringing as near to perfection as is possible their every ability.

However, resistance to learning can offset the best of all plans and structural configurations.

From experience in industry, it is obvious that if pieces of metal are identically processed, the resultant pieces will be next to identical having only an extremely small measurable variation.

Conversely, groups of students identically processed in a classroom situation will end up with vastly different degrees of accomplishment. Each has a different experience base upon which to determine value. Each listens differently. Each interprets from a unique perspective. Obviously, people are unlike the non resilient pieces of alloy that can be treated reliably measuring up to pre-determined quality standards.

Is it okay that each student finishes up in school different from every other student? Why not? Is diversity better than sameness?

Then, why is so much effort put into making each student the identical of every other student? Ah, is it some false founded self-satisfaction derived from all having the wherewithal to pass a test? Is it truly nobler because as proclaimed we want for everyone to have the same common denominator?

As understood, even without direct experience, a stone that

cannot be made into a good car engine piston might be made into a magnificent component of a fireplace. Likewise, some students that cannot be developed into certain highly technical components for the marketplace may be developed into contributing members of one of the other valued aspects of the social enterprise be it social worker, gardener, house builder, musician, or artist. Simply, the total of all of the assets of every student need to be brought to perfection for the benefit of all. It is what each deserves leading to a better life for self and everyone everywhere.

Without the appropriate disposition of the students, the realization of a good school is impossible. Students must be as willing as they are able to participate and learn.

Consequently, a good school by any measure seems to be proportionately dependent upon the students who happen to converge from a neighborhood or who are enrolled from families not necessarily of financial wealth but importantly of riches valuing workmanship and personal wholesomeness. Most of the students that congregate in these recognized schools are there because of their community perspective. These students could probably learn on their own without the aid of teachers. If left uninhibited by the school system, if left alone to rely only on their own resources, they might likely achieve as much or possibly more.

On the other hand, some schools are comprised of students who tend to be reluctant perhaps because of inherent developmental shortfalls in combination with demoralizing and self-depreciating learned behaviors. For these individuals, the challenges may appear to be insurmountable. The schools may mirror their disabilities. Yet, if under some set of circumstances if certain issues could be remedied, if attitudes and dispositions could be positively modified the characteristics of a good school might emerge enabling at least perceptible learning gains. Thus, the ingredients of a good school may require more than a generalized set of directives.

A school that could enable learning as well as improve student dispositions might be more than a good school. It might qualify as a fantastic school, even a really great school. Some schools have achieved that standard.

These should be regarded differently than those schools that are likely to be classified as "good" having attained some measure of notoriety only by the number of three and four star advanced placement or honors courses they offer. Some schools gain recognition for offering a coveted "blue ribbon" curriculum whatever that is.

However, is this not for the select capable few top level students within the school of three schools in one? Is this not misleading since all students do not participate equally?

Often it appears not to matter then that a good school truly meet the needs of everyone in their population. What appears to matter is rather some achieved label derived incidentally to real purpose.

From experience, students who have taken the high-end-only-for-the-very-best-student classes may indeed have been misled. Often their proven skills and abilities indicate that these so-called high powered college level or college equivalent courses were still high school after all.

Students have said, "I already know all of this. I had college level anatomy and physiology in high school."

With exception for their surprise, after one or two weeks into the course of a college taught anatomy and physiology, they often acquiesce voluntarily.

Certainly, a good school is some combination of many elements in various proportions arguably, even the number of advanced degrees held by the faculty. But, schools can be even better than good when with all of the intangibles in place in humility they serve the very specific needs of the attending students and thereby the communities that they support.

The true test of a good school then is to take its students whatever their wherewithal to where they could not otherwise arrive. A good school can only be so recognized for that difference it actually makes rather than for what it might proclaim as student status, competitive rank, or in the accumulation of awards. Thus, a really good school without any recognition or notoriety may be at work in obscurity.

A good school can only emerge if it has the courage to look within itself to assess its attributes, determine what it specifically contributes, and to evaluate the differences it makes. A good school has to research itself, to analyze what it does. It has to be internally accountable. And, it has to be committed to make needed changes to get the desired results for the very specific community that it serves.

Incidentally, why use the term "good" school rather than possibly "great" as applied to a school. Actually, good is good enough. Though great would be the ideal, in most cases just getting to good is a steep hill to climb. Within its structure, a good school should have the ability to inspire, motivate, and provide insights that are the groundwork for success in teaching and learning, for doing its job.

A good school through its dynamic configuration brings change within a nurturing community. For those students who mature more quickly, opportunities need to be available that will enable their expedient continued growth and development. Regardless of age, they need to move on to the next higher level of opportunity. Provisions need to be made for them to continue their academic advancement without restriction. Let them go on if they so choose.

For others, a different sequence may be in order. Some schools do offer co-op, the opportunity to attend school and work part time. A portfolio of the work experience is kept so that school credit can be earned. However, in addition to such work opportunities more than just job shadowing should be available. Trade organizations need to make available entry level apprentice programs. As well, students should have opportunities to work in community service and in association with humanitarian organizations. All can enrich maturing individuals.

In collaboration with local schools, one company in the Midwest developed a two year training program in manufacturing technology. Fifteen selected students entered the program at the beginning of their junior year. The immediate goal was to teach basic engineering in the process of building simple robotic machines. They did!

During the course of the program, students developed skills in blueprint reading as well as basic drawing and design coupled with electronics and machining. They used manual as well as computer controlled lathes shaping various parts and tools that would be needed as assembly line machine components.

A secondary purpose was to recruit students. Upon graduation from high school, those with notable skills and motivation were offered either talent matching jobs or presented with conditional scholarships in support of college and university degrees.

Today, in some communities, early college for those ready students is beginning to be advocated. As is the case, this is an idea whose time finally has come. But, it was a disregarded idea twenty-five years ago when my daughter at age sixteen still in high school began taking college classes.

In place of superfluous high school electives, she was given permission to leave her modest high school, drive to the nearby college campus, participate in a class or two, and return to complete her high school day. Nobody had heard of such a thing before and often with a grimace or frown scratching their heads or stroking their chins some would react, "You said what?"

By the time my daughter had completed high school, she had earned twenty-six transferable college credits. Three years later, she would graduate from a reputable university with a bachelor's degree including a double major in International Business and Political Science coupled with a foreign language minor.

Her younger sister was not as fortunate. Denied, she had to slug it out through four years of high school that led only to nothing more than a diploma, no opportunity for academic advancement. Her high school principal said, "We have no provision for a student during the school day leaving the campus even to participate in college classes." Some agreed, "It was out of shortsightedness. It was too innovative. It was unconventional. It might grow out of control."

What can be surmised? Is it agreeable that if a student were capable, accommodations should be made so that their efforts in development would be uninhibited? Is it agreeable when minds are ready to move on, they need to move on? So, why is it not feasible to move high school students on as they may need?

Which of the two schools attended by my daughters is the "good" school?

Clearly, the high school attended by my younger daughter was not into the concept of making accommodations as might be needed.

They could have been helpful not only for my daughter but as well for many other students and very likely could have become a pacesetter in developing new and meaningful trends in secondary education. That was in the late 1980's.

Flexibility is required for good schools to advance their students as quickly as possible thus eliminating or at least reducing self-depreciating boredom and lackluster dispositions about school that by hearsay may find a way into the attitudes of other students. In general, schools need to do something more for their students than hand down the heritage, they need to measure up to needs.

Area colleges and universities should be amenable to forward moving high school students. High schools, colleges, and universities need to collaborate in the service of education making possible every opportunity for every person. The heretofore exceptional should become the commonplace. Preventing this are the man-made obstacles, essentially an assortment of excuses. One is student age and another may be rooted in a false sense of superiority exhibited by the prerequisite requirements.

Is that acceptable especially in the marketplace of today?

While that may be okay for those who want to pursue a prescribed degree, what about a person who because of life experience feels capable of signing up for an advanced class in accounting or a law school course in real estate? Why deny anybody?

Sometimes, it seems that institutions of higher learning are inclined to fabricate restrictive and limiting barriers that enable self-admiration of accomplishment while prohibiting the opportunity and advancement of others. It seems that the individuals that manage these institutions become self-inflated as they create impediments for others. Instead, consistent with Darrow's counsel, they should be unassuming in those accomplishments. They should be looking for satisfaction in streamlining all opportunities.

One community had the audacity to set up a novel institution, a lifetime learning center. Its purpose was to mediate the training and development for the already employed and to help those in transition to quickly develop new skills for placement opportunities. It was state funded and it was structured to rely upon the assistance of existing community colleges and universities. However, wanting it all, those in higher education could not tolerate the presumed competition. Over time, these pretentious leaders forced the demise of this worthy advancement in learning, an experiment that might have led to a continuously upgrading, adaptive, and knowledgeable workforce.

Do not be surprised. "Johnny come lately" organizations now have adopted by accident, surely, the concepts and methods of this forward looking forerunner organization.

Importantly, why did something good even worthy have to be destroyed? Should it not have been promoted? Was it out of ignorance alone or some artificial bias?

If individuals have been left behind for whatever reason, let them have even novel opportunities to recover. Allow individuals to have access to training and development programs as needed when needed. If young people in schools are impatient in getting on with their life, make it possible for them to move on. Permit these exceptional students to advance more quickly in higher level academic pursuits even by alternative routes.

Is that not better than imposed confinement in an unyielding system that can only be justified by age and time constraint grouping? Who can say?

Recall the young lady cooking ham for the Thanksgiving dinner. What we always have done out of habit or by some hand me down action is no longer good enough.

Industry developed the expression, "Think out of the box." Advancing education does not even require that much effort, perhaps only modesty and a willingness to be helpful without excuses or deference to some higher power as a state commission on education.

When it needs to be done, find a way to do it. Then, do it.

In summary, the good school gives hope and inspires optimism. It is the one place that takes students from where they are to somewhere beyond what they might otherwise have achieved. It lifts them higher and enables the establishment of dreams with their conversion into reality. It instills noble qualities, enriching character and facilitating a resourceful lifestyle. It is made from within through its own initiative to make self-assessments, to develop a self-knowledge, and to strive for the continued enrichment of its strengths. A good school is more about substance and the realization of its purpose than it is about cosmetics and glitz. It abides by a philosophy that subscribes to doing what is right for others by doing what is right.

The difference that is made in the life of a student by a group of caring professionals is what now gives credibility to a school. The understanding especially shown by teachers determines notable outcomes and the measure of that care and understanding is at least in part the measure of a good school. Really, it could be so much more through the implementation of augmentation efforts that set aside the existing impositions and constraints.

Why do students return to their schools of graduation? Do they come to see the secretaries or the counselors or even the principal?

Usually, they return in the acknowledgement of an exceptional caring teacher that made a difference. Of course, this is a subjective point of view and not easily quantified.

Would it not be remarkable if the care and understanding elements could be translated into a quantified and meaningful tool for assessment? Could that really happen?

Without question, if schools are to improve and if outcomes are to improve purposeful restructuring is inevitable. Ideally, the transformation will put in place a master teacher with differentiated staff leading the processes in exchange for the essentially independent teacher system predicated upon the principal as chief administrator. As well a caring disposition and flexible configuration acknowledging student potential would make an enormous difference.

Certainly, principals were perhaps good teachers and these individuals may have thought that by taking a leadership position in the schools they could make a difference. On the other hand, they may have become disenchanted and even dissatisfied lacking the needed chutzpah to continue in the classroom. They may have thought, "As hard as I try nothing will ever change. Enough is enough. I have to get out of this classroom situation."

Admittedly enabling advancement and matriculation into the social structure must occur at a pace that is both motivating and accommodating. When ready, students need to move on to the next stage of opportunity.

The bottom line is that change is needed and mandated by the current shortfalls in performance. A new approach is required even if only experimental. This seems to be a reasonable assumption.

In the very beginning, at the moment of commitment to create a good school, a set of uncompromising core values defining the essence of purpose must be established. More than a mission statement, other than a list of goals or objectives, it embodies the totality of correct attitudes, acquiescent dispositions, and certain work ethics.

It will be the driving force. It will set the beliefs that firmly establish focus and permeate the operations of the entire organization. It will be the preamble by which the school will be recognized. Only upon precisely defined elementary and idealistic building blocks will habits of excellence emerge.

Conceivably, set of core values might be written according to the follows:

We will be the best at what we do. To that end we will:

- Establish the leading edge of teaching innovation that maximizes learning while respecting and encouraging the initiative, curiosity, creativity, and personal well-being of each individual;

- Serve the needs of our constituency by fostering the environment that promotes a disposition amenable to the development of essential habits of excellence;

- Act conscientiously cultivating individual responsibility with a focus on integrity and high ethical principles that define Good Citizens of Earth; and

- Provide a foundation for problem solving, critical thinking, and prized abilities and skills applicable in the marketplace.

Furthermore, we will set ourselves at the forefront establishing the model of a learning organization in education.

In that, it is agreed the school needs to be:

- driven in its quest for quality performance;

- upbeat and positive so as to promote inquisitiveness, the likely foundation for the valued and highly regarded qualities in the marketplace; and

- intent upon forming important common denominator skills of understanding and interpreting data, assessing and summarizing information, essentially analyzing, evaluating, prioritizing conditions and circumstances that are predicated on at least the basic abilities in every form of communication as well as mathematics.

The external pressures from the well intended "No Child Left Behind" legislation will likely change little in education except perhaps to lower the level of achievement for all. In general, schools will likely continue to do what they have always done and consequently will continue to get what they always got. As established in contrast, schools must become learning organizations, introspective and self-evaluating focused upon lessons learned that will lead to substantive and real improvement.

What is likely to happen is beginning to occur; noncompetitive students are one way or another for one reason or another exiting the system. They realize the path they must take. It is out of the ivy covered buildings either to drift away going nowhere or waft into some alternative program that as often will lead them to a dead end.

Regardless, for one reason or another, one way or the other, these students are no longer on the academic books. School wide achievement scores on some arbitrary test will go up. Shouts of jubilation will be heard everywhere. Good for the administration but not so good for society. What will have been accomplished?

With other described elements in place, one of the problems in part can be resolved with a series of lessons and presentations set into an individualized instruction format for any student within a group.

In a group, as incredible as it may seem, while a clear purpose is in mind, each individual in the audience will receive the message as they may have been conditioned. The words and materials may be the same for everyone. However, incorporation for each of the individuals will be as unique as each is.

While the inclination may be to think of that as strange, it is the experience base and the subtleties in the dispositions of each person even thought shifts from moment to moment that result in variations in the development of different kinds of mental residence. Thus, a lot of work needs to be done to determine if instructional materials and methods are overall working properly. A critical part in making the assessment is having designed appropriate evaluation instruments for the selected delivery vehicles.

Many questions need to be asked. Many answers have to be discovered.

Are the evaluation instrument items congruent with the specific objectives and the outcomes they are intended to achieve? Is the means for achieving the respective objectives spelled out as a do-this-to-get-that plan? What provisions have been made for students who may fail to get the concept? What repairs need to be made to the presentation or to the assessment items? What environmental adjustments need to be made? What other kinds of analysis should be going on? Is there any "kaizen," a plan for continuous improvement? What is it?

Putting all of this together and teasing out the nuances is what teaching is all about. It is what makes teaching exciting, interesting, and intriguing. After designing and implementing the selected instructional strategies, the evaluation instruments become the indicators of success and the gateway for revisions as needed.

The master plan influenced by the core values gets broken down into manageable segments and possibly units to be subdivided into lessons of the week or day whatever is suitable for instructional management. Recall, the overall scope of the school should be in the development of marketplace-ready Good Citizens of Earth.

Generally, in schools, the lesson plan has served as the backbone for the from-start-to-finish presentation of subject matter. For it to have real substantive value, a lesson plan can only be developed over time with careful and thoughtful analysis. It is more than a goal or objective followed by a list of what the teacher does and what the students are to do in addition to whatever presentation equipment and materials may be needed. It must be a carefully structured collection of strategies that will be vigilantly studied and revised repeatedly until it functions as a reliable map leading to intended preconceived and essential learning outcomes. It should be all about what teachers do to get desired student achievement. Ideally, it would be collaboratively coordinated and ever changing.

With well formulated lesson constructs, schools can develop a means for quality control and systems analysis patterned after what has served industry for several decades.

W. Edwards Deming set forth fourteen quality control principles that changed the entire manufacturing industry. Many of these principles are applicable to education. Certainly in teaching as in industry, schools must strive for excellence and the outcomes must be no less than excellent. The applicable quality control principles that may enhance school products can be summarized as follows.

- Define the work of necessity, allocate resources to do the job of teaching, and be alert to improve the design of that instruction. Budgets should be adjusted in accord with the attainment of the proposed instruction.

- Rework of any kind commonly in the form of "extra credit" and "outside work" assignments cost more in effort than the "inside work" done correctly the first time. Here we need to change the "superstition" that any performance at the moment will do because the work can be done again and perhaps better at a later time. Of course, that is a supposition that is unfounded. What is demanded of students is all they can ever be or will ever be. The bottom line should be and always must be achievement at the highest level.

- Develop individual independence and self-reliance. And, develop a "do-whatever-it-takes" disposition to settle for nothing less than perfection, the very best sincerely.

- Constantly improve the system of learning and study. This begins with intent and an inclination to develop more and more efficiency and effectiveness in all aspects of student workmanship.

- Supervise well the work that is assigned and encourage pride in workmanship as a reward in and of itself.

- Provide the setting where students can be successful by removing inhibitors to good workmanship.

- Eliminate all elements of fear that may be associated with performance, participation, and evaluation.

- Encourage habits of teamwork as a means for achieving success. Students need to learn to unselfishly help each other succeed but only with integrity in effort. They must learn to set aside all decretory behaviors.

- Work to eliminate scolding, the use of clichés, exhortations, and nagging in every form as well as setting up what might be regarded as artificial and arbitrary goals or rewards.

- Work to eliminate the "quotas" that impede quality, reduce productivity, and demoralize attitudes. Utilize only meaningful and substantive assignments rather than the ho-hum "busy" work that can fill a period of time.

- Carry out programs that encourage learning and lifelong self-improvement. And, put into place strategic methods that include a cycle of planning followed by implementation and revision as indicated by evaluation and accountability systems.

From fifteen years of experience in auto parts manufacturing, the application of quality control principles makes sense. Every process step has a specific purpose. Every action is designed and structured to get the desired result. Every element is set up to assure the production of parts that are within the acceptable range of tolerance. Flaws, defects, and variation by whatever practical means must be eliminated. Nothing is taken for granted. Poor performance cannot be excused. Livelihoods are at stake.

Without the benefit of this experience base, my research studies utilized the same pattern from start to finish. It is appropriate now as it was then. Later, working on a National Science Foundation project, a consultant from a prestigious school of business was required to offer suggestions as well as evaluate and approve procedures and processes. After spending a day together discussing all aspects of the project, the consultant left with only these parting words, "You don't need me. You're doing just fine on your own. Call me if something changes."

Schools need to emerge with the same perspective.

Some schools may never be able to measure their products on a six-sigma scale of perfection (that is fewer than one part in a million has an unacceptable flaw) but operating with the proper tools and the suitable mechanisms in place, schools may be able to enable students to achieve at the highest level of their potential. Should they choose, school systems can produce worthy, noble, and substantive contributors to the marketplace.

Remember, with few exceptions, "any subject can be taught to any child in some honest form" (J. Brunner, 1963).

Schools need systems analysis plans of engagement that will carefully track their effort while pointing out strengths and weaknesses. While they may be inclined to work on the weaknesses, schools must have a commitment to "hold the gains" operating with a focus upon their strengths. Schools must get into the business of managing the best conceivable teaching and subsequently the highest level of learning.

Schools and their teachers need to develop a system for instructional program management. This is likely to be a network of sequential interrelationships linking each step in presentation and evaluation. It must be a system of controlling variables and it needs to be predicated upon deserving objectives that have been defined after a substantial up front needs assessment.

A typical plan may be patterned after the following:

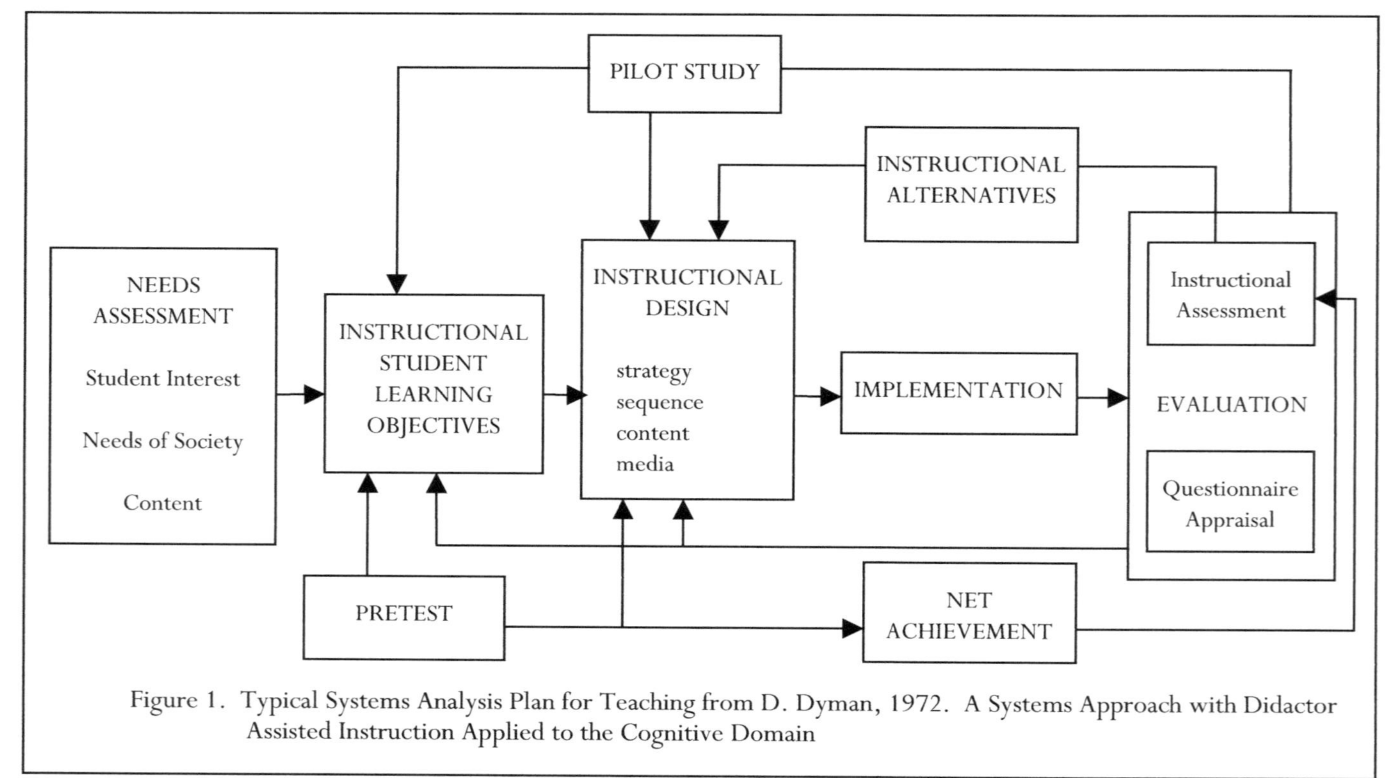

Figure 1. Typical Systems Analysis Plan for Teaching from D. Dyman, 1972. A Systems Approach with Didactor Assisted Instruction Applied to the Cognitive Domain

Obviously, elements depicted in the Systems Analysis Plan for Teaching may be modified, some taken out while others added. All elements need to be carefully documented and placed on some kind of flow chart as the instructional lesson is mapped out and planned.

It must be emphasized that the evaluation instruments must be congruent with the objectives. With the right instruments and tools, assessment of outcomes will provide appropriate insight on the impact of teaching by way of knowing both the starting and ending points. Often in developing these instruments, subtleties may alter the perspective and affect results. Care must be taken.

Evaluation feedback for students and teachers is different. The need to know outcomes for teachers may be protracted. However, to have value, students need to know immediately the outcome of their performance. They need to have immediate correction for every misunderstanding. The more proximity, the more significant will be the impact upon learning especially when the goal is mastery. This had been substantiated by the work of both Skinner and Pressey.

In planning, teachers must always be thinking in terms of the needed marketplace skills always thinking in terms of what students will need when they reach the next level.

27

When thinking about the marketplace that one way or another every individual enters sooner or later, "think out of the box" always comes to mind. That says a lot. But, a lot more needs to be said.

The marketplace is where everything happens and surely if asked, everyone would have some kind of thought or insight about the meaning of that "where everything happens."

Generally, it is the place where dialog and transactions take place, where business gets done, and where industry operates. It is the arena of every conceivable interaction. It is the environment where interchange among individuals occurs that enables the distribution and trade of possessions in every imaginable form including money, goods, services, and conversation. It may be as small as a neighborhood or as large as the world itself. It is the system into which everyone contributes and extracts. It requires no less than earning your way.

In the marketplace, a lot of what happens does so through organizations in one form or another: government agencies providing regulations as well as an array of public services, business and industry that make and exchange commodities perhaps from food to weapons, and schools as well whereby the heritage is handed down as it is with the potential for continued exploration, discovery, and invention.

The marketplace demands that curiosity is kept alive and thriving. Progress is built upon derived innovation. Consequently, this seemingly fragile quality needs to be in place, sound and well. Schools, the crucibles of teaching and learning, out of necessity must provide the substance for inquisitiveness that sustains as well as contributes to all advancement.

For sure, the well-being of a curious mind is likely dependent upon early childhood experiences even before the time of school but teaching techniques need to be in place that unlock the potential and provide for the nurture of its many positive facets.

PBS (Public Broadcasting Service) at one time presented an in between programs snippet, "Stay Curious."

At two o'clock in the morning in a darkened bedroom an alarm clock awakens a young girl who arises from her bed fully dressed in plaid shirt, jeans, and sneakers. She slips out of her house, hastens across a field to a chicken coop, and there as she peers in raises a bright light that shines through a window. A rooster begins to crow. The girl turns away and begins to smile.

How wonderful is a moment of great satisfaction?

It seems that if behavior is always confined with rules and regulations and inhibited with fear eventually interest will break down. Curiosity will disconnect and the claim for identity will take on the form of mischief or outright unruliness. Children and young individuals need to be participants and permitted to fail and even break things as that may still lead to positive outcomes.

Playthings are given to enable imagination and as may be necessary taken apart to "see what makes them tick." Sure, it may be upsetting to have a child pull off the arms and legs of a doll or to rip the wheels from a truck but these growing minds want to know how things work. They even trek away to a favorite place and cut their hair or crayon the walls. Adults need to rely on the ability to laugh and maybe even cry. They must realize that a "mind is a terrible thing to waste."

If youngsters were already behaved as adults the need would no longer exist for this destruction that inspires the mind to search for truth, to wonder about the heavens, to explore even around the next corner. Certainly, it had been the visions of visiting Mars that inspired a young boy, Robert Goddard, to build rockets that one day did propel Viking 1 and 2.

Unfortunately, the curiosity of most adults is already in a box resting on a top shelf perhaps in a closet. It is the place where special toys and gifts are carefully tucked away and kept so that they would not be broken prematurely or at all. There preserved by thoughtful and well meaning parents for a later date when a child would be older, wiser, and appreciative of those little treasures that by then may be of no interest. These actions out of admirable protectiveness are stifling.

Importantly, curiosity branches into many other wonderful definable qualities including: creativeness, ingenuity, imagination, innovation, and resourcefulness.

In school and at home and through various organizations and youth groups, youngsters on their way to maturity need to be encouraged to make things and do for themselves putting ordinary things together in extraordinary ways, ultimately, to learn about how things work even about how society works together and sometimes apart.

One teacher with whom I had worked deserves considerable regard. Yet, he will likely never receive any recognition. He encouraged his students to build Rube Goldberg type contraptions. It involved sequencing a series of operations that ultimately perform a simple task; for example, releasing a steel ball that rolls down a track that trips a paper clip hook that springs a rubber band that spins a wheel that closes a switch turning "on" a light bulb.

The motivation does not come with a sign or label that reads, "Do not try this at home or in school without supervision."

The idea is clear.

The paramount academic abilities can only exist if interest prevails, if a "go-for-it" or "try-it" attitude has not been stifled. It is a willingness to become involved without the trepidation of some scolding or reprimand or of the humiliation of failure.

It seems that the bottom line is to keep threats and anything in any form that diminishes self-worth out of the equation for helping children grow straight and tall with confidence. Contrary to what some may think and believe real humility is embedded in knowing true worth firsthand. It is the real high ground of life.

Youngsters growing into maturity will find themselves and know the extent of their true worth. Others need not impose any limitations as well intending as they may be. Parents and teachers collectively with everyone in the community need to be uplifting and encouraging.

During my time as a Materials/Operations Manager, I met a young lady independently supporting and nurturing a toddler son. She knew the pain of having been scolded and ridiculed. She vowed that no matter what the situation or circumstance she would never resort to name calling or self-worth denunciation of her child. She adopted the playful word "silly" as a refrain when all did not go well, when things were dumped on the floor, milk was spilled on an outfit, or an accident occurred. She would try to make little of the incidents and she would say as a reassurance, "That's silly," and then smile or laugh so as to imply, "It's okay. We can clean it up. We can fix it."

Her perception merits admiration.

Many good and solid personal qualities are needed to enable all of the marketplace systems to work well. The successive business fraud scandals that have been endured demand truthfulness above all. Integrity can never be undervalued. The notion that business is amoral is an excuse without merit.

Reliability is also at the top of the list of desirable qualities. It assures confidence. On that certainty, the future can be planned.

In some parts of the world, trust is essential. Business is conducted on the good word of another and sealed with a handshake. Some communities have developed such a high regard for self and reverence for another that theft of any kind is unthinkable. Anything lost and found is returned to its owner exactly as it had been recovered. The reward is in returning the item to its rightful owner or by making that possible by placing the item in a community lost and found center. It is true.

Tolerance, patience, and enthusiasm are the qualities that set aside differences guaranteeing that whatever the job may be, it gets done as it should be done.

As well, time management and self-management are coveted.

Parents in addition to teachers need to expect timeliness and understanding by demonstrating their own command of these perhaps virtues. In other words, "if I can do it, so can you." Leadership actions do send a message louder than words just spoken in a command.

Knowledge, the ability to recall mentally stored information is good and it does have purpose but for those without a wholesome capacity, encyclopedias have been constructed and search engines have been fashioned to store and maintain this wealth.

The use of knowledge, the ability to understand or comprehend information, is well beyond the ability to simply call to mind. It leads to accomplishment. It is exemplified as knowledge becomes useful. Thus, it is of a more lofty order than fundamentally the ability to summon up "factoid" entities. It is consistent with the phrase, "two plus two equals five." The whole becomes greater than the sum of the parts. Bits of what is known can be manipulated and rearranged to provide new insights and relations that expand the bottom line. It is a prerequisite of "thinking out of the box."

Students must be given a reasonable amount of information and they should be expected to interpolate and extrapolate making associations within reasonable boundaries. Expect that this transition will require patience plus a measure tolerance and test scores will show clearly that representing comprehension is more demanding than representing acquired knowledge.

The critical skills are application, analysis, evaluation, and synthesis. They are provisions that result from processes of the mind and grow out of fundamental curiosity and true worth awareness. They can be developed only through opportunities as offered by way of thoughtfully planned instructional systems.

Application, an ability of higher order, involves the use of abstract thinking to deal with a variety of situations. It is the ability to "know" three for example without the presence of apples.

While some notions associated with abstract thinking have fallen along the way, maturing youngsters should be given opportunities to work in the abstract domain of thinking and reasoning. It requires visualization of processes without the presence of the concrete items. It is the cognition of shapes and dimensions apart from models. It is the ability to "see" with the "eye" of the mind.

Perhaps the transition from the concrete domain to the abstract can be facilitated by asking youngsters to visualize as if seeing as does the eye of a whale in navigating the ocean or a hawk flying in the sky in search of a mouse. Maybe this ability develops when maturing individuals are asked to see whatever may be their interest but with their eyes closed.

Analysis enables an individual to break down a report into its basic elements in such a way that the parts can be placed into a hierarchy of significance or that the implications from within can be clearly grouped into categories and explained or even rearranged into a new whole. For example, analysis leads to deep and rich perceptions of procedures and processes as they apply to desired outcomes. It uncovers the intricacies and shades of assorted interactions so that resolutions can be forthcoming, a pattern can be discerned and associated.

This progression is critical in dealing with complexity because it enables the critical examination of every ingredient, part, or fragment in such a way so as to enable qualified predictions including thoughtful and deliberate actions supported with confidence based logically upon findings. It is critical to problem solving. Its roots may reside in the destruction of toys. Who knows?

Let students take things apart even if it is a poem. Have them truly work with the pieces and then reassemble them into new fashions. Afterword they might write their own questions and discover answers beyond what may have been defined as their reach.

Evaluation should be obvious. Basically, it involves the qualification and quantification of elements associated with a problem. It has to do with assigning value to the various and meaningful components and then making trade-off decisions. It makes use of predetermined criteria and the application of specifications. Everything needs to be weighed and assigned some denomination of worth perhaps to consider the color of red as it presents itself in a painting of a partly cloudy sky at sunset.

Lastly, synthesis is just that. It involves pulling together all of elements, combining them into a meaningful whole whether it is for a memo, an operational plan, or the derivation of an abstract relationship.

It can be developed through writing a report or a research paper. It hinges upon taking the students one step at a time helping them connect the dots to see the whole picture. It is a lot like baking a cake, building a birdhouse, flying an airplane, getting a ledger right, or adjusting a machine to make good parts. It is about doing rather than watching.

Ultimately, it is about putting it all together whatever it may be. It is about getting results, good or bad, that then can be scrutinized coupled with learning to hold the gains. It requires re-implementing the work with readiness to do it over and over again with a focus to achieve at the highest level even perfection if that is possible at all. The big "thing" here is achievement predicated upon holding the gains.

The life's fantasy of Robert Goddard confirms that. He never lived to see his boyhood dream become a reality but only because of his persistent effort did "we" land on Mars. His boyhood experiments in rocketry led the way.

In the process of developing the various marketplace skills, realize that not everything needs to be found on some blueprint or ledger sheet pertinent to some business or industrial operation for a student to grasp and develop these skills. But, having command over the wherewithal enables the elements to be found at all. It is about recognition and discovery leading to problem solving at its best.

While it is hoped that students graduate with fluency in the use of these skills, they are not taught in just a single subject. They need to be taught in coordination across the curriculum in every class at every level as they can be taught. And, as can be accomplished, these skills need to be encouraged for use beyond the doors of the classroom and surely beyond the outside doors of school itself.

All of this implies a consensus among teachers ideally led by the efforts of a master teacher working with and through a structured supporting faculty.

Of course, the marketplace requires that all of its participants are able to communicate in mathematics at least at the level of setting up and solving basic ratio and proportion problems including per cent as well as collecting and presenting data in basic tabular and graphic forms. Ideally, students will have a taste of algebra and some experience in geometry.

Computer literacy is essential. It is beyond playing games and keyboarding basics. It includes the use of the worldwide web tools in all of their forms.

Lastly, participants must be able to communicate attentively using input skills, listening and reading, and fluently by means of output skills, speaking and writing.

The community of residence and beyond into the global marketplace needs well prepared young people to address the issues at home and abroad. They need to understand their place in the environment and value their impact as Good Citizens of Earth.

28

While we often think in terms of reading, writing, and arithmetic, students need to be led to develop the foremost skill of communication, listening.

"You shouldn't leave home without it!"

Perhaps most people can adequately read and write. They understand the ramifications of the written word in script or print. Within this framework, individuals have the potential to understand as well as to be understood. However, they need to appreciate the realm of the audible. They need to understand the difference between to "listen" and to "hear."

Like reading, listening is an "input" skill. Before all others, ironic as it may be, this skill of listening is the first in use. Possibly it is the most essential of all communication skills. Unfortunately, it is without regard and is at best just assumed. It is more than "to hear."

That listening is the foremost skill is evidenced in the behavior of parents talking to their newborns hoping for a response. It is a reaction to sounds and even a reply to the unspoken word, body language that comes with "goo-goo" and "tickle, tickle" that may be accompanied by an assortment of facial expressions along with a beaming smile not to mention bounding head and shoulders coupled with motion filled arms and hands.

The sensory perception of hearing is by nature different from listening. Though confused the words are used interchangeably. Hearing is the auditory response to sound waves transformed into nerve impulses that make their way to the brain for interpretation.

More than the stimulation of nerve endings following several mechanical steps, listening requires the use of active mental energy that interprets and evaluates sound received through the ears. It requires "attentiveness." Thus, a difference between the hearing of a sound and the mental processing of the sound, listening, does exist.

While students are inclined to say, "I'm listening," as part of what might be perceived as a successful multitasking effort in reality what they are saying is that they are recognizing the existence of sounds while attending to another endeavor.

During the course of a classroom presentation, say to an apparently distracted student, "Are you listening to me?"

The common response is, "Huh, I'm listening. I hear you."

Upon questioning to assure that information is correctly received, the student may be able to repeat some or all of the words just spoken but is absolutely unaware of their combined meaning. The student has not processed the sounds into a thought that can be paraphrased or converted into some action. Simply, the student does not understand. Essentially, the student mind was "turned off" or "tuned out" by some predominating diversion, likely copying homework for another class, thoughts of a meeting after school, or a jump shot to win a basketball game.

Who knows? And, a plea to listen does not get it done.

The root of the problem is in another domain. Perhaps it is indifference caused by a worn out and tired disposition from the same old thing day-in and day-out, that is school.

This cannot be moderated, fixed, canceled out, or set aside with "hands-on" activities that are viewed by some as the answer. In effect, these diversions may well dilute effort rather than lead to wholesomeness. They are a kind of appeasement or distraction, some kind of amusement that somehow has been connected to learning some concept, though requiring more time, and is therefore an acceptable practice sometimes even praised. An example might be cutting paper strips that are turned into loops connected in chains that represent the hereditary molecule.

Oh, my! In high school no less.

As two masters cannot be served at the same time, the mind cannot "multitask," listen and talk or daydream at the same time. Simultaneously neither is done well. Likely, it is the listening part that is underserved.

The importance of listening is evident. Countless costly mistakes are made because the listening effort fell short or did not occur.

Why is it that the skill is not meaningfully considered within the realm of communication skills? Why is it that listening, the most basic of skills, is neglected in deference to reading, writing, and speaking?

Shortfalls in listening are most likely the significant obstacle for learning and for appropriate actions. So, to assure that learning has a chance, the primary upfront skill that needs to be developed is dedicated attentiveness as needed when needed.

Most of every day is involved in communication with approximately forty-five per cent of this time used in listening. For students, between sixty and seventy per cent possibly as much as eighty per cent of the day depends upon listening.

While individuals ought to be good at it, most people have a relatively low proficiency in listening with a fifty per cent memory failure rate immediately following a ten minute presentation.

Maybe the predisposition toward listening underperformance begins during childhood, when dialog is usually one sided, when input into conversations is prohibited, when a youngster might say, "But, Mom" and, gets the reply, "Shhhhh."

The tendency is to find circumventive ways into the system or give up. The common descriptive phrase is "turned off" after being turned away.

People with urgency and persistence have the tendency to get their "two cents worth in" to most conversations. So, listening stops in anticipation of a break or opening into what is being said. During this wait, the verbal reaction is being planned. The second master is being served.

Another reason for poor listening is that individuals develop a notion of comparative worth. Consequently, personal biases and values often interfere. Listening is tempered by these personal and self-imposed projections.

Boredom as recognized by the periodic interval response, "uh huh," is a relevant clue that what is being said is already understood and patience is just nobly being granted or maybe the intention is just to appease.

Mental and physical fatigue can be a deterrent to listening as is ordinary daydreaming that has been linked to the primary culprit, the difference between the language processing rate of the brain and the rate of the spoken presentation.

Note that the word processing ability of the brain far exceeds the normal speaking rate. The gap between thus enables the mind to drift from input. Obviously, speaking faster is not humanly possible consequently more commitment must be put into the mental processing of words. A disciplined will is required to overcome this waywardness.

A person can be expected to mentally process in excess of 625 words per minute, perhaps even 800 to 1000 words per minute but typically speaks at a rate of only about 60 to 70 words per minute. This difference most certainly permits mind wandering and the infiltration of an array of mental distractions. Overcoming this deficiency with practice can improve listening performance.

Out of shear interest, I once purchased a variable speed tape recorder/player. Amazingly, the rate of speech could be increased by fifty per cent. Gradually, as the rate increased, focus intensified and comprehension comparatively improved not unlike the results that are obtained as reading speed is developed and increased.

The bottom line is that individuals need to ably listen to the spoken word forming congruent mental images. Then, in turn respond. The facility in listening is paramount in creating an atmosphere of harmony within and across relationships throughout the marketplace.

The desire must be to listen, to mentally follow along with devotion.

Acknowledging the proverb, "Let me be eager to learn and slow to judge" makes a lot of sense. It is predicated upon listening.

If listening development does not occur in school, then when and where will it occur?

Teachers and schools do try to do a good job with reading, writing, and speaking. However, they usually fall short in reading, the second most important of the communication skills.

During a visit with my granddaughter, I noticed that her reading manner was contrary to everything that has been recognized as the way it ought to be done.

Her mom immediately rebuked my recommendations saying, "That's the way they are taught and she doesn't need to be different in school. Anyway, her teacher will insist that she should learn to read as an adult without pointing to the words. More so, she doesn't need her classmates laughing and making fun of her."

Certainly, all of that may be true but that is too bad.

Obviously, this skill is impaired by the way reading is presented in elementary schools. Through the early habits that are put into place under the banner of "reading as adults" young students grow to get the same results. They learn to read slowly, that is, poorly.

It would be great if an otherwise five hour reading assignment could be completed in just two or three hours and with improved recall.

Why do teachers insist upon methods that damper the process?

In either the first or the second grade and now in some schools as early as kindergarten, the children are forbidden from placing their hands under the words they are asked to read aloud. This prohibition and method of sounding words has two negative impacts on adult "silent" reading.

First, by not allowing the hand to glide under words as they are read, eyes tend to drift across the page and backtrack seeing again the words already read, a kind of stuttering. This ineptness slows down the reading rate considerably.

Recall that the mind can process in the neighborhood of 625 words per minute and perhaps a lot more. Should a person read slower than that, the individual will have "time" for mental wandering. Reading may even become laborious at best and boring at worst. Their response may be, "I don't like to read."

Second, as students are asked to read aloud to help them with pronunciation for good reason, they develop the habit of mentally speaking the words that they read. Thus, they are limited by the rate at which they mentally talk to themselves, approximately 60 to 70 words per minute, ultimately reading at a rate of 125 words per minute. Essentially, youngsters "learn" to read only as fast as the "little voice" of their mind permits. Then, because their mind is not fully occupied with the written word, it is "free" to be diverted to other thoughts. Thus, they may become distracted as they read so to say, multitasking.

Studies do confirm that a hand on the page as a "pacer" during reading pushes the eye movement forward and enables more rapid reading. Using this technique can almost immediately double the reading speed of course with a little practice. These studies have shown that this "hand on the page" technique leads to increased comprehension. Without any surprise, recall improves probably because less mental time is available for distractions.

The typical reading aloud exercises that prohibit rapid processing of words should be judiciously limited. As well as can be achieved, students should be encouraged to more rapidly process written words that flow to the mind through their eyes. This is important.

Television snippets encourage children to read and even encourage their parents to read to them. They should now encourage children and parents to read more efficiently and effectively so no one will chide them or laugh when they do.

If this has been confirmed years ago and makes sense, why is it not practiced in schools? Is it that reading teachers need to be retrained? Are these teachers and schools behaving as the young lady cooking Thanksgiving ham? Should reading teachers become teachers of listening as well? Would that be remarkable?

Where would that begin? Should colleges and universities become the starting places? Should this be encouraged through government agencies by legislative act as soon as possible? What will it take to put reading and listening improvement measures into place?

Is it possible to change from what has been in place for countless decades? Is it reasonable to agree that educators need to look into this matter, that they work at developing methods that will improve competency in listening and reading, two essential skills for learning?

By the actions of schools and teachers, one of the essential skills for learning is taken for granted and the other is being mishandled. However, the notion of win/win does remain possible.

29

By default, students need to be taught the skill of study. Study is other than memorization. It is a process that leads at least to understanding or equivalently comprehension as a result of building linkages among and across particulars. Concepts formed from elements become bound in a web like network sometimes referred to as mind or concept map. The concepts enable "seeing of the big picture." Study requires the reasoning abilities; analysis, evaluation, and synthesis, connecting the "dots" in the formation of interactive models and ideas.

The emphasis in schools seems to be placed on memorization but then, if that is the thrust, how do students recognize the need to be resourceful, imaginative, creative, and innovative?

These qualities are the backbone for pushing the frontier. They are the essentials within the marketplace. They may be summarized as "thinking outside of the box" or thinking at all. Considerable effort needs to be placed here to encourage the development and application of these natural abilities.

Textbooks and notes serve as foundations for the acquisition of information in most classroom settings. These items especially books need to be seen as real tools not unlike the hammer or the saw of a carpenter. This idea comes from an encounter with a college friend who would rip pages out of a book in anticipation of what he might be able to read while on the bus en route to school. Interestingly, as he read the pages, he would then throw them away.

"Why?" I asked.

He replied, "I don't need them anymore."

That approach is not recommended but the notion of not saving a book is worthwhile. Books should be used and consumed not unlike tools used by any craftsman. Books should be annotated and cross referenced. Notes should be written in margins and across diagrams. Books should become totally personalized for and throughout study.

When I was in high school, textbooks were issued "free" for student use but, at the end of each academic year, the books had to be returned without any writing or extraneous marks. Teachers checked every page. Vividly, I can recall the dreaded process.

Students would line up in front of the teacher's desk. Patiently, each would wait until it was their turn for book inspection. The teacher would go through the book page by page. If a mark were found, the student would be sent back to their desk to erase it. Then, the student would return to the end of the line to quietly wait again. It was so very monotonous.

The solution was simple though it might not have been smart. Others, as I had learned to do, just did not use many of their books. Books stayed in the locker just as they were when they had been assigned. Gloating non book users would not have to face the peril of standing in line again and again until the book would be cleared for use for the next school term. Consequently, books were never used as the tools that they could have been, that they are. Students were never positioned to understand their usefulness.

Years later, while in college classes I did come to recognize the value of taking notes during class lectures and then faithfully would embellish my textbooks with margin notes and an array of reference links. This facilitated study from interwoven working resources. My understandings improved considerably as did my grades.

Today, to augment textbooks on loan for student use, "Post-Its" work well. Students position them where needed and fittingly record their notes. Books can be fully used but are not marked up or blemished. They retain their maximum value in the resale shop as well should that be their ultimate destiny.

However, from another perspective, a book may cost $120, only a few dollars in comparison with the tuition and fees for a course.

Why not use the book advantageously until it is consumed yielding absolute benefit?

Books are precious for the thoughts that they contain and the freedoms that they represent and insure. They are not in short supply. While expensive, they are not cost prohibitive.

After using a hammer and saw in building a house, those tools might need to be replaced for work on another project. Certainly, in building a house, a carpenter would not think to either save the hammer or the saw thereby forfeiting the greater good, the house.

Why should a student think to save a textbook and shortchange the maximum of a learning opportunity?

And, the work of neatly copying notes that were hurriedly taken during the time of a classroom presentation should be considered as a useless effort. I have met students who do copy their notes so that they will be tidy and organized.

As a youngster, I was boldly encouraged to copy and rewrite notes. Oh, my notes were perfect.

Later, I would remark, “So, what.”

By well intending teachers, I had been misled. Perfect notes did not equate to perfect understandings or to perfect test outcomes.

All too soon, I realized, “Why bother with the notes. Adequate is good enough.”

The note copying task amounted to a purposeless use of time and was essentially mindless. Precious moments were consumed for the sake of a painstakingly written page in which I was to take pride while good academic insights considerably more important were falling by the wayside. Learning that translates into ability is what matters most and that at least could render acceptable grades.

Rather, students should be encouraged to embellish their class notes as may be needed using their textbook and available resources. Cross referencing does work.

The act of adding to notes or complementing a textbook during a time of recall or "debriefing" is extremely important. This should occur as soon as possible after the notes were taken. Debriefing limits forgetting.

The military use debriefing exercises quite well. After a mission, individuals are presented with countless questions about what they had experienced. Eventually concepts expand yielding new insights. Improvement is possible.

Also, relying on text or other materials to fill in gaps enhances concept development. Learning can take place from a package of shoddy appearing notes that have been worked over with crucial references and added information. The process is interactive.

If clouds remain even after a best effort, those points should become the questions at the beginning of the next class encounter.

Several years ago, a success story was published about a person who without any previous industry experience purchased an airline. The article described the new owner as standing over a large table covered with ledgers and process sheets coming to grips with the details and particulars of every element of the business.

Picture this person, shirt collar unbuttoned, sleeves rolled up.

Perhaps students should take on a similar profile as they study rather than the relaxed feet up on a desk with book cradled in their lap likely listening to favorite pieces of music.

To get the idea correctly in their minds, to get into the "right" mental framework that study is really hard work, students might try studying while wearing work gloves. That would be a switch. On occasion, I have recommended that technique. None, I am sure, had followed up but maybe the suggestion was at least eye opening.

Another doubtful practice that is common among students is to write out outlines and develop "flash cards." At first, both might seem to be worthy efforts enabling the commitment of information into memory but in effect the aimless copying over minutes and perhaps hours adds nothing well at best little to learning.

In the first moments of study, students often go over the details of information as they construct their "study tools," perhaps an outline. Unfortunately, as they get closer to the test time, they tend to skim over their self-made study materials. They become more and more superficial. They rush through no longer attempting to connect with or access the details.

The last moments are actually less productive than those spent up front but it is on these end reviews that recall relies upon most. This is perhaps why when taking a test, students often realize that they are familiar with the material but cannot differentiate among the details provided in the options. I had this experience. I gave it up.

Some classes do require memorization. For each term of an organic chemistry class, I had taken enough class notes to cover nearly two reams of lined notepaper. All had to be memorized.

In response, I used marker pens to write reactions over and over again across the pages of available out of date newspapers. I could not afford the cost of otherwise reams of paper. I would scrawl big sloppy letters and numbers without regard. It did not matter if any of it were legible.

As I performed this almost daily exercise, I would talk my way through the reactions. The practice secured the ability to recall necessary details but contributed little to comprehension. Today, disappointed, I can recall some general ideas from the course and only a few of the countless "factoids" of information. I would rather have developed meaningful interlinked concepts that I might have retained.

Instead, developing the big picture up front is essential. Afterward, students need to fit in the significant details and bits of information. With each addition, the framework will expand and become more inclusive.

Study should be more like an artist painting a landscape. Gradually, the picture evolves beginning with a pencil sketch on canvas, continuing with the application of color, and concluding with fixing the details.

Commonly, study is the other way around. Facts and details are noted at the onset and subsequently blurred in the sketch of the concluding outline.

Should students reverse the study process or look at it from another perspective? Could this be why many students cannot write in depth about what they had studied?

If compelled, an outline might be seen as the trunk and branches of a tree. The flash cards could be added as leaves representing the details that could be embellished. Even so, as they study, students need to mentally ask a multitude of questions weighing the significance and interconnectedness of the material at hand as it flows through their mind. Students should focus on trying to develop a bigger and more elaborate detailed "picture" as progress occurs.

Although, if understanding is the required goal as it should be, from experience, nothing helps more than teaching. With confidence most first year teachers have affirmed this.

In one college class, during weekly small group meetings, students were asked at random to teach some aspect of the previous lecture class material. All had to be prepared to stand up in front of the others of the class and simply explain a part of the lesson. Their grade depended on it. They did it. In time, they became believers. It is in the involvement that learning occurs.

One of the most important requirements of study is to finish on time. Students err in their tendency to study for as long as it may take without any time constraints. This practice may lead to malaise and possibly complacency.

At the onset of study to ward off lapses of any kind an assessment should be made about the time that may be required for the effort in relation to the time that actually may be available. Students should judiciously limit study time and they should set a time frame in which the work "must" be completed. Only then with a prioritized time line in place should they set out to accomplish their various study tasks.

With practice, students should be able to develop the skill of time management that also will minimize the stress so often associated with study. Time management is the key to effectiveness and efficiency.

In contrast with college or university students, those in high school ought to study in class with teacher supervision and assistance. That would be more meaningful than the often no recourse mental groping tactics that might occur during unattended study efforts likely in the corner of a bedroom.

More than once, I had worked with students who demonstrated what I described as "deflective study behavior." One such student, married with a young child, was in an anatomy and physiology course. Her test scores were poor overall.

After she had taken a couple of tests with only marginal scores, I said to her, "You are capable enough as I have observed your work in class. What seems to be the problem with your test scores?"

She replied, "I don't know. I guess that I'm just not good at taking tests. I always study the night before."

"That's a classic rationale" I thought as I inquired, "Describe what you do when you study, every detail. How did you study last night?"

She answered, "Well, after the baby went to sleep which was about eight o'clock, I laid out my work on the kitchen table. It is comfortable for me there."

Impatient for an answer, I interrupted, "So, did you use your notes, your book, what?

Looking a little hesitant, she responded, "I used both my notes and book. And, I usually make a list of what I think is important. I concentrate on those items."

Again, I cut in, "That sounds reasonable. But, could you have omitted something of importance from your list though trusting that it to be complete? Just as well, please continue."

She went on, "You do know that I'm a mom and I have things to do beside study."

"Explain that," I replied.

She added, "Well, before I could finish all of my studying, I did the dishes and tidied up around the house so that we would start fresh in the morning."

"Oh," I said.

She listened intently, as I added pleading for her understanding, "But, couldn't you just study and tidy up after the test? What difference would a day make? The priority before you was the test. You have only one opportunity to study but you have a lifetime to do the house work. You do understand that."

Finally, with her eyes focused looking up from her work space, she nodded indicating that she had understood.

However, I doubt that the next time she had set aside the housework and with a thorough list studied to capacity as she might.

Many students excuse themselves from their number one job with alternative jobs that also appear as maybe equally important. That cannot be criticized yet it does interfere with the task of study and learning that would last throughout their life and most likely secure course credit and eventually lead to a degree and successful employment.

It might be said of them, “They had their priorities mixed up.”

Resistance is another impediment for learning. Frequent enough, the root of this is in attitudes that have developed from early on perhaps caused by conflicts of one kind or another, likely involving parents, teachers, or both.

However, can anything become accomplished if resistance of any kind is present?

Students and their teachers, once students themselves and who should now be students of a higher order, are of course human representing every known quality including the power of choice that embraces dereliction or disregard. Refusal is possible. Most of all, youthful students may not have the maturity to accept what may be deemed “best” for them. The intention for learning must come from within their disposition.

The mind must be inclined. That is the way for it to be.

Attitude that inspires enthusiasm determines the outcome of every human endeavor. Our perceptions of ourselves are foremost because in any endeavor, a person cannot give what they do not have.

Poor self-perceptions will continue to lead to poor results. These in turn lead to reinforcement of previously held erroneous beliefs. The cycle goes on and leads to an ever diminishing benefit. At some time and in some way the sequence must be disrupted so that positive results may be achieved and sustained.

How does a less than needed disposition come about?

Most likely, the self-image of individuals is formed long before anyone had previously realized. Self-perception and self-esteem may be carved out before children are three years old with the likelihood of earlier than that. For good or bad, dispositions can be altered by any input from others in the home or within learning environments.

If a student hears only criticism or if a student comes to realize that their performance is less than that of associates, they may begin to develop self-doubt, they may begin to grind away at their self-esteem viewing themselves as "junk," and they may increasingly dislike their circumstances. The perspective needs to be set aside. Encouragement can make a difference. Motivation is a primary behavioral change technique.

Those who see themselves as successful and gaining in praise tend to be more positive about their self-image and tend to be more willing to take on learning risks. As they continue to receive praise their self-perspective may then progressively spiral them upwards. We are what we think we are.

30

In the second grade, a little girl was forbidden to talk with her best friend throughout the school day and unbelievably, she was forbidden to speak to or play with her little pal even during recess and lunch.

Something is wrong with that. Is it mental cruelty?

As a consequence, the little girl began to fail in class. Certainly, she was stressed and exhibited consummate symptoms. However, within a week, in a different classroom environment, the high performance of that child had resumed. Her workmanship was equal to the best in the class. As important, her behavior again became that of a happy school girl, the consequence of teacher wholesomeness.

Prior to the sixth grade, her parents had moved to another school system. Again, this now petite school girl would be besieged with difficulties. Her assigned classes were: English, mathematics, social studies, and metal shop.

Yes, she was placed into a trade shop class. She would be the only girl in a class of boys with a curriculum that included the basics of soldering and even welding.

According to the principal of that school, she was a transfer student without proven standing in the new system.

Why working with steel? Why not home skill, craft classes, or art and design? Why not something more suitable for a young lady?

After some parental haggling with the principal, with reluctance, the young girl was transferred into sewing.

That was not the end of it for her. Early in the school year, during a class assembly, she along with the other youngsters in the sixth grade were told by the principal that their poor behavior qualified them as the worst class of students in the entire history of the school system.

How is that for a rainstorm in your life that cannot be comprehended nor reconciled by an eleven year old? Is that too much to mentally process? Should a child have cause to lose heart and even personal direction?

Imagine a more disturbing way to begin a school year. Fortunately, she and the other students of that sixth grade were mentally tough enough and fought back. They held on to their self-esteem.

Over the next seven years, many of these budding adolescents achieved higher recognition for success in school than all previous classes.

At the high school graduation ceremonies, those elected to speak in behalf of their classmates reminded their former middle school principal and several scornful teachers as well that they had not forgotten the category in which they had been placed. They were unwavering in the face of the encountered negatives and refused to think less of themselves and that having succeeded with self-determination plus a spirit of optimism they were about to move on to a brighter future.

Why should students have to cope with their teachers and administrative personnel? Is it reasonable to expect that the work of school administrators and teachers should be focused upon upgrading and uplifting achievement rather than diminishing it?

Could it be that at least some school board members had been confronted with and confounded by destructive incidents as well but have been unable to rise above as did the little girl and her sixth grade classmates? Could it be that the animosity of some board members toward teachers is at least in part the result of some residual perplexing school experiences perpetrated by nonetheless licensed personnel? Is any of this excusable?

However, is it reasonable to expect that those belittlers in charge of schools could do no less than the group of mistreated but prevailing and honorable children who demonstrated the will to overcome the shortfalls in their school experience?

Their position demands it. They should practice, "Treat others not as you were treated but as you would want to be treated with dignity and reverence if not at least respect. Above all, practice to do what is right because it is right. Be noble in your responsibilities."

Children cannot understand abuse by those they intuitively perceive as caregivers. It is an inconsistency that cannot be mentally reconciled and is overall regrettable.

We must understand the impact that any series of negative encounters might have on the disposition of students and their willingness to cooperate in learning activities.

Should youngsters in any grade in school have to learn to deal with their supervising adults? Should it be the other way around? Can it be conceded that a single incident let alone a series of degrading confrontations would most likely result in a diminished response and a sense of abandonment? Is it true that how an individual thinks determines what that person can achieve?

Generally, we think in terms of winning or losing. Nevertheless, winning fourteenth place may represent a fantastic effort.

Who might think it? Then, is coming in second really losing? How about coming in last? Should individuals begin to think differently if they were last? What if they were last among the most outstanding or moderately outstanding? Among the commendable is last disgraceful?

In every class someone must accept the reality of the last place. That place is and always has been reserved for someone.

Unconditionally and without qualification, is it okay to come in last? Does place really matter that much or matter at all? If place does matter, what place becomes at least acceptable? Is place a comparative issue?

Presumably this notion of place especially in school needs to be evaluated.

Often in school, because the experience is protracted over several years, students look to the end as their only goal. They look to see it over and to get it over. That becomes the paramount focus and the focus seems to intensify as students advance through the grades.

I know firsthand. I have witnessed it every day over several years of teaching.

As every successful person, the proverbial road begins with a dream. Astronauts and Olympians as well as many top level executives have begun their careers with a dream. This somehow needs to be instilled in the children in every school. From an early age, students need to write out their dreams be it poet, postman, politician, cab driver, trash collector, mountain climber, baseball player, birdwatcher, or stargazer. Every student has to see that through learning in school they can achieve their dreams.

This may be difficult but certainly it needs to be put into place. If not many, some students in even prestigious universities are not certain about what they want to achieve.

Then, why pursue a degree?

The often heard response is, "I'll figure it out as I go. Maybe something will come up."

What will come up?

This is an example of kidding yourself. Schools need to provide for the exposure that will enable youngsters to begin to realize their dreams and act upon them.

Many years ago, when in the third grade, my oldest daughter came home with a note from her teacher who wrote, "Your daughter is daydreaming in school. Her time would be better spent concentrating on school work."

Probably, a moment of daydreaming here and there would have been acceptable but this daydreaming as described seemed to be a significant obstacle to her success in school.

As a well intending but ignorant parent, my daughter was summoned to appropriately respond to her work in school. She was encouraged to set aside her daydreaming practice. Presumably, the problem was resolved. No further communication on the matter was received from that teacher.

As I have reflected over the years, my admonishing action will be regretted forever.

How could I have made such an imposing mistake? What precious thoughts might I have stamped out through the beckon of her third grade teacher? Was my daughter dreaming of the stars, the excitement of traveling to new places and beyond, or of other great and wonderful adventures?

Schools and their teachers need to encourage the daydreamers and help their students set hopes and fantasies into a plan that may take them to places they might otherwise never know. Schools need to assist youngsters to understand their purpose in school and the benefits that they can derive from being positively involved.

Students then may have the insight of how each day of work accumulates and contributes to the attainment of each and every goal. They may take on a new contributing attitude rather than looking only for an end.

Is that reasonable? Is that possible? Should students be led to develop a variety of personal lifelong skills that generally are prized in the marketplace? Should they be led to develop a positive sense of true worth, that they are a composite of qualities, skills, and abilities that individually and collectively have merit? Should they be led to understand that their sense of true worth can be enhanced or diminished by their own thoughts and that their sense of worth is transmitted to others by their actions? Should students be led to develop a sense of desire that will enable them to strive for and achieve the goals that they have set for themselves? Should they be led to know that their desire must be more than a synonym for want?

Apparently, before seeds can grow into the acquisition of standards, the dispositional soil must be properly prepared.

Students need to be led to develop an intense focus and thirst for something that is noble and worthy of effort. Coupled with the desire to achieve, students need the confidence of self-belief that daily provides the platform for "moving mountains."

Harold Geneen, former CEO of International Telephone and Telegraph, once said,

> If ordinary mortals can scale extraordinary peaks, so can you; if you don't, it's because you either didn't want to or didn't work hard enough.

And, from Helen Keller,

> I am only one, but still I am one. I cannot do everything, but still I can do something. I will not refuse to do the something I can do.

Belief is the lever for success of every kind. Its source of energy is determination the will to try, to never quit.

Students must understand that they are responsible for their own initiative. They need to understand that if they do nothing, they can only achieve nothing. Only if a goal is set, lofty or not, if a workable plan is laid out, if attainment can be conceived, initiative is inspired. Desire may emerge. Striving for self-improvement needs to become foremost and routine. Teachers should encourage this acquisition.

Along the path of every endeavor courage is essential enabling persistence in the pursuit to face the challenges without excuses but rather with the resolve to measure up. Integrity may be required in choosing the appropriate options. Helpful associations with others may need to be established. The practice of tolerance that embodies patience and open mindedness may have to be developed.

Lastly, students should have command in self-management. That is the bottom line. Applying acquired knowledge in doing the right things in the right ways at the right times is paramount. Appearing appropriate on every occasion is essential. Making yourself attractive to others is crucial.

These are among the essentials that may lead to well balanced young adults who have had the opportunity to frequent the schools in a quest for learning and self-improvement. Anyone or all of these can be derived or squelched by way of the positive or negative motivating efforts of teachers.

31

It does seem reasonable that the middle eighty to ninety per cent of the students in high school most likely can master or develop respectable competency in any subject.

What prevents this from happening?

Is it from the beliefs derived from previous experiences including subconscious inclinations of self-image that hold students back?

In all probability, the degradation of self-concepts begin early and are due to the errors in the teaching and learning processes caused by ill founded parental methods and an array of inept practices within the context of teaching individuals in groups.

It is a "no-brainer." How individuals are treated leads to what they become.

What can be done about the abandoned child, the disillusioned child without parental support or perplexed by over aggressive parenting, the little girl who could not talk to her best friend, the young man who was lost in math progressing one page after another not having mastered the previous page or pages, and the daydreamer daughter who was sanctioned? What was the impact of these unfortunate experiences?

Once while preparing dinner, I was alerted by the little boys next door, screaming in the backyard. Noticeably, tears were streaming down their faces and stomping their feet, they were pleading, "No, Daddy. No Daddy."

The boys, ages five and six, were being encouraged to sleep together overnight in the tent that had been set up in the backyard.

The father was saying, "You'll have fun. It will be like camping out."

He repeatedly assured the boys about the adventure.

During the encounter with the boys, the compliant mother offered encouragement, “Try it. Try it. You’ll be fine. You’ll see.”

The boys would have none of it.

In apparent frustration, the father placed his hands into the armpits of the oldest boy and forcefully pushed him into the tent. Immediately, as he could, the boy ran out now frantic, sobbing and screaming, “No, no. Please, no!”

After a few moments, the mother went into the house to return with a lantern that she placed on a nearby picnic table. She affirmed, “Don’t be afraid. Your father and I will be outside. We’ll be here to watch during the night.”

The children were not consoled. They continued to hysterically beg to be excused from the presumed terror of being left alone in a tent throughout the night.

After a few more attempts to persuade the children, the father took both boys under an arm, one in each hand, and shoved them into the tent, oldest first. Now, visibly angry, he zipped shut the passage.

While the boys cried, the parents played a card game on the picnic table keeping their word to watch. Until late into the night, the children would sob and plead. With persistence in crying and begging, eventually, the children won the right to sleep indoors.

Notably, these parents were upright in the community. They were held in high esteem by the neighbors and no one would be inclined to question their parenting credentials. Nonetheless, at least once these parents, well intended as they may have been, traumatized their children. Did other similar distressing moments for other noble justifications take place in the confines of their home or in a store, restaurant, or playground?

In another situation, a boy of five, sitting on the floor of his room among many changes of clothing was overheard repeatedly saying, "Why do they have to make it so difficult for me?"

It was a Sunday morning. The family was preparing to go to church. The child was asked to wear his dark pants with a blue shirt but he preferred wearing his jeans with a yellow baseball shirt.

Was he building a platform of preconceived notions that no one likes or cares about him that unfortunately might be displayed as an outburst at a later time or lead to some reflective behavior showing disregard for others? Was he not programming his subconscious? Was he not creating mental images that later might be unleashed resulting in negative realizations.

How we treat others has a powerful impact upon the shaping of their thoughts and upon subsequent actions.

After some negotiation, the matter was amicably settled. He would wear his choice of clothing from among alternative options. He went to church in a finer cut of jeans wearing the blue shirt. A compromise was achieved.

Later that year, at Halloween time, he was asked to wear a coat over his costume to keep him warm on a cold evening. He cried desperately pleading, "But, Mom."

The situation was explained to him but he insisted.

As if to confirm, we do sometimes hold the gains, his mother thoughtfully said, "Please think about this. It is really cold outside. I want you to enjoy the evening but I do not want for you to get sick, to miss school, and to play with your friends. As you have seen through the window, other kids are wearing coats over their costumes. Please go to your room to think about this for a minute. You do have two options: choose to wear a coat and be able to go out to enjoy the evening or choose not to wear a coat and stay in the house and pout as you might."

After only a moment, no doubt realizing that he was missing out on the festivities of "trick or treat," he emerged with a smile wearing his coat. His choice earned a hug and praise that filled his smile with delight.

Would he have gotten a hug and praise if he had decided to not wear a coat and stay in the house?

Of course from this mom he would. The reward would be for making a worthy choice.

The idea was to offer options and enable a decision making process selecting from among possibilities that were available. The decision was left to him. Either choice would be acceptable without reprisal. As desired, this approach did lead to a happy ending.

Some students are likely to have been poorly influenced by their companions. One such student in a class assigned to me boasted saying, "Yeah, after one party, my mother still can't get the puke stains out of the sofa and carpet."

When I met this individual, his grandmother had taken on the burden of rehabilitation and she seemed to have had little impact on his behavior. His inclination was to be intentionally spiteful.

Others along the way have associated with gangs and for their satisfaction display a "tough guy" kind of behavior. One brazen and rebellious individual over time persuaded several other students in a class to refuse the efforts of their teacher. Their grades began to spiral downward to match his resistant performance.

Do the fearful moments and unfortunate experiences that youngsters have even into adolescence impact their future trust with others and especially with teachers in school? Will it have a carry-over effect on teacher relationships and studies in school? How many are distracted by not well intentioned associates? How many individuals as these can be tolerated in a classroom before teaching is negatively impacted and learning is degraded?

What can be said about teachers? Were some similarly affected at least by a form of abusive parenting? Would some as well have had to enjoy a dad and mom imposed "good experience?" What might be the classroom backlash effects of this kind of imposition? Would these teachers with a background of self damaging experiences cause really wonderful children to hide under a table? Or, might their teaching style prohibit learning in other ways?

On another occasion, a different neighbor was cleaning up yard debris after a storm, a fallen branch from a tree. He whistled sharply. Within seconds, his is son came running out of the house.

Is this not an interesting way to summon a child of thirteen? Are many sons or daughters for that matter inclined to answer to a whistle as an option for being called by name?

Perhaps rather than call students by name should teachers whistle to summon their attention, of course, only if that is customary at home?

Students so demeaned might be encouraged to notify the teacher, "Should you need my attention, please whistle. I respond to a whistle."

Should it be that way? How do you reverse the impact of a whistle that repeatedly suggests a subservient self-worth? Does a link exist between performance as well as behavior in school and the manner by which a child is summoned by his or her parents?

Jokingly, one comedian tells that he had thought his name was "Damn-it" until he got into kindergarten because when his mother would call for him she would say, "Damn-it, get in here!"

In contrast, what might be the method to move a person to a positive cooperative self-concept so that learning might be accomplished? Ultimately, could it be an effort in futility? Could it be that the more effort is put into bringing about the change of an imposed disposition the more resistance may be encountered? Is any of this conjecture verifiable?

While on a field trip, one of the students began to behave disruptively, repeatedly striking a tree with a fallen tree branch and thus caused a sequence of loud cracking noises. Other students became distracted as the park ranger spoke to them about forest characteristics along that part of the trail.

Out of frustration realizing the students were inattentive, the ranger blurted, "You are the worst group of students that I have ever taken through the park."

Upon returning to the school, the student had been reprimanded by the principal. He had been ordered to run laps around a one quarter mile track until exhausted, an interesting punishment.

Could this student have "learned his lesson?"

As he ran, what might have been his thoughts with each step?

Was the voice in his mind repeating expressions of disrespect and self-domination so that after completing the demands of the penalty his disposition would be worse than before?

Certainly, the student learned that he could survive a wearying ordeal. He may well have realized that his bad behavior would bring to him no more than the equivalent of an endurance test. He may have recognized that he could overcome any such imposition and go on. He could remain adamant.

Likely, this kind of punishment led only to a deeper undisclosed disregard for authority. He may well have reinforced his resentment because nothing about his behavior did change.

While working through a lab activity that required a series of related arithmetic calculations, I noticed a girl just sitting, staring.

I inquired, "Are you okay?"

She snapped in reply, "I don't know what we're doing! I can't do this. I'm not good in math."

She never did make any progress even after reasonable but not overly imposing assurance that the work was within her grasp.

Stubbornly, she refused, "No, I said! I can't do it."

I felt that until then we had a positive classroom working relationship. Her refusal said, "No, you are mistaken in your perception."

I thought, "Continued coaxing might only cause her to become more entrenched in an already deeply unyielding disposition."

Consequently, I said to her, "Should you change your mind about this, I'll be here for you."

Why did this young lady behave in this self-depriving way? What caused this, a "bad" experience at home or in school?

A few moments later, on the other hand, another student did comply after being mentally nudged.

At first he reacted using the same expression, "I can't do this."

The response that he got was the same, "Yes, you can. You can do this!"

After several moments of refusal countered with encouragement that enabled the presentation of an alternative version of the problem, he responded, "I do get it. I do get it now. I can do this!"

During this elated outburst, I looked over to the girl to see if now she might have weakened even slightly yielding in her point of view perhaps thinking, "If he could, I could, too." But, her posture remained stubbornly fixed and rigid.

In addition, what can be said about the "time out" kids?

One student in the hallway outside of the art room was painting a "Time Out" stool. The stool was to be offered at a school auction.

She said as I passed by, "Hey, what do you think of this?"

I was a bit taken by it because it was truly thoughtfully done. Various timepieces and clock faces as if ticking away where painted in a collage on the seat that presumably for good measure included a stack of dog eared well worn books and ruffled homework papers set into the background.

I replied, "It's beautiful but it's not right."

Astonished, she inquired, "Why?"

With a smile, I said, "Though your creativity is great and the stool is indeed imaginative, we shouldn't be promoting 'Time Out.' It gives kids the opportunity for negative mental reinforcement that can lead to resistance and other frustrated behaviors."

Looking a little puzzled maybe because she was anticipating a career in teaching, she said, "I never thought of that."

Not too long after that, I received a call from my oldest daughter who as soon as I said hello exclaimed, "Guess what!"

I replied, "I can't."

She went on, "For quite awhile I didn't see Hilary or John and neither did I hear a sound from either of them. Out of curiosity, I quietly went looking for them. You'll never guess what they were up to."

"No I can't. You will have to tell me." I replied.

She continued, "They pulled a table in front of the closet

doorway, put a wooden box on top of the table, and then a chair building a makeshift staircase that enabled them to climb to the top shelf where I store books and toys that are too advanced for them."

"Hold on," I interrupted with a chuckle. "If they can build an access to some stowed away books and toys, they seem advanced enough to be able to have them would you agree? But, more important now, tell me what did you do?"

She answered, "Weren't they clever? But, of course, I couldn't tell them that. So, I scolded them for climbing in the closet and gave them a 'Time Out' as a reprimand."

Before she could say another word, I interrupted saying, "Wrong."

"Wrong? What do you mean? Didn't I do the right thing?" she said.

I answered, "Think about their thoughts as they sat for however long in 'Time Out.' They likely were upset that you had punished them for their ingenuity."

"Yeah, I see what you are saying but how do you show them so that they should not do things that can lead to their hurting themselves?" she replied.

I answered, "Perhaps, you take a doll and drop it from where they were standing for them to see that they could have fallen as well and that they could have gotten hurt. Remember, you don't want them to seed negative thoughts.

After letting them see the danger, you might go to the hardware store then buy a lock that you use to keep them out of places as the top closet shelf until they are old enough to better understand. This way, you become a "teaching" mom rather than one who is seen perhaps as nagging and impeding. Isn't that what you would prefer?"

The reply was, "Yes, you have a point. I'll try that."

Is that reasonable?

As well intentioned as it may seem "Time Out" is a punishment, less strenuous than running until exhausted but it still enables the one being punished the time to think about the imposed situation, usually as they may perceive it "for no good reason." As they may pout and ponder, their thoughts may sprout the roots of future resistance and possibly an assortment of negative and devious behaviors.

During my first year back in teaching I had the privilege of meeting a young man who was enrolled in a class that appeared beyond his reach. When this became obvious, I arranged for him to share lunch with me.

As we ate together every day, I would tutor him for thirty minutes more or less. From time to time, we just talked. During one of these moments, he revealed that his father had abandoned him and his mother was again using drugs. Both had found their way back into jail.

He said, "I have it good now. I have a place to stay. The people I'm with take care of me."

The people were elderly non relatives who gave him an upstairs room. Oddly, these people had raised his mother who too was abandoned by her parents.

He had every reason to be discouraged and rebellious. Instead, he was docile and grateful.

"Why?" I often wondered.

Before the semester was over, he would be transferred to another school district where he could receive more appropriate legislated learning assistance. Hopefully, this young man will go on with a positive sense of self.

In contrast, many students have been formed in non confrontational, non-humiliating, wholesome, as well as valuing environments. These are young ladies and gentlemen who are positively enthusiastic. They are pleased with themselves and they wholeheartedly accept their circumstances. They exhibit confidence and certainty in their actions. They are comfortable about themselves. Offering a positive circumstance should be the goal of everyone nurturing children at home or in school.

32

The bottom line that determines every human action depends upon the thoughts that are consciously and unconsciously harbored.

James Allen (1864 - 1912) wrote the hallmark piece, *As A Man Thinketh*, on the impact of thoughts over actions.

> Man is made or unmade by himself; in the armory of thought he forges the weapons by which he destroys himself; he also fashions the tools with which he builds for himself heavenly mansions of joy and strength and peace.

Thus, if thoughts are changed then behavior is changed. Certainly that is easier said than done. Of course, in schools, the right thoughts are the bottom line for success as they are in business and in life in general.

Is it possible that everyone needs to do a little reflection on their behavior and the thoughts that they keep?

Several years ago, I put together the series *Think and Achieve*. It was an attempt at challenging and changing behaviors. As it had been conceived, it was a program that incorporated the practice of visualization coupled with a self-accountability system patterned in accord with the method that molded the character of statesman, Benjamin Franklin.

When the work was given to a friend for review, he said, "Let me tell you a story about this."

His story went like this. While out filling his car with gasoline, he experienced some frustration with the way the pump was operating and became more infuriated when others nearby offered suggestions.

He said, "On arriving at home, I reflected on the incident and realized that my poor choices and my behavior in general were not representative of how I see myself to be."

With a vertical line down the middle, he divided a sheet of paper. In the left column he wrote a series of single words and phrases that described his behavior at the gas station. In the right hand column corresponding with each of the words or phrases to the left, he wrote a counter word or phrase of how he would like to have been. Then, one by one, he read the right hand column statements into a tape recorder.

At the close of each following workday, when he arrived at home, he would play the tape recording at a low volume so that it just was masked by the music that he would normally listen to.

He proclaimed, "After thirty days, I was none of what I had written in the left column and all of what I preferred to be in the right column."

While that may appear a little far-fetched, that is exactly what happens day in and day out as minds are programmed, surely the subconscious dimensions, with reactions to events as they unfold. Frustrations or joys are mentally embedded and they are positively or negatively reinforced each moment. The mind confirms feelings, "Yes, that's the way it is" until some eye opening event emerges that alters convictions about the environment and the people in it.

Predicated on the thoughts that are kept, individuals anticipate, wrongly or correctly, events before they actually take place. They prepare themselves for future events that may or may not even occur. As if attracted by a transcendental force, they work themselves into the anticipated situations. They color their visions with hues of rose or blue and they tend to react as they have programmed themselves to be. Human beings have this astonishing quiet power that renders equally negative as well as positive outcomes. Generally unaware, human beings have the capacity to choose their behavior by the thoughts in which they invest.

Most disconcerting is that the possession of this awesome subconscious power is not typically recognized. Also, it is unacknowledged that not only are behavioral patterns put into place but that those already in place are being reinforced or disarmed.

All of human actions one way or another are built upon some kind of self-assembled externally influenced foundation. Certainly teachers and parents need to understand how their repeated actions influence the thinking and behavioral patterns of youngsters.

Recall the expression of the five-year old boy, "Why do they have to make it so difficult for me?"

How about the young man who had been punished by having to run laps around a track until he had become exhausted?

What might have been his thoughts with each step from where he started out until the place where he had collapsed from fatigue? Could they have been anything but accusative and counterproductive? Could he have thought, "I'll show them!" and begun the development of a deeper resistance to school and others associated with the endeavor. Or, was he committing himself to reform. It was not likely a resolve leading to improvement. A few weeks later, the behavior of this young man became even more incompatible with the social structure of the school. He was expelled. In that, he may have achieved his hidden desire.

Teachers and parents need to be aware of their potential impact in grooming, shaping, and programming the emotional and behavioral dispositions of children and adolescents in school.

Several years ago, on my way to work I would pass a small tree, maybe ten feet tall, that had been pruned into the shape of a football goal pole. On at least one occasion, I thought, "How clever. Remarkable!"

Sometime later, when preparing for a growth and development training program, I went back to photograph the tree as an example but it had been cut down.

Then, I thought, "Too bad. It exemplified how by our thinking, perfectly good trees can be trimmed into something though novel that is in reality a distortion of what they were meant to be. Similarly, children are shaped by our interventions that are not always good for the recipient."

As with saplings, youthful individuals are most vulnerable to mistreatment, irresponsible, or inadvertent frustrating behaviors imposed by the "pruning actions" of others.

Do impositions inhibit curiosity, stifle creativity, prohibit resourcefulness, or limit inventiveness?

Is it reasonable to believe that individuals are born inherently curious? Is curiosity good? Should curiosity be accepted of course with some trepidation even when the curious are exposed to risk as were the children searching the top shelf of the closet?

What if a well intending teacher sent a note to the parents of Robert Goddard? "Your son is daydreaming during class." Or, what if the teacher wrote? "During class, your son is doodling, making sketches of rockets."

Is curiosity the fundamental disposition that enables learning? What mental destruction may result from the continuous stifling of interest from the continuous use of worksheets? Will children and adolescents develop a "give up" or "whatever" attitude?

That children and even adolescents get into stuff may be annoying but it seems that the "right" needs to be protected. Curiosity must be encouraged especially early on when the mental "windows" are open for assimilation, when a child wonders, "Will the rooster crow?"

If from time to time, punishment seems to be in order, it needs to be structured to promote learning and encourage alternative behaviors to do what is right because it is right.

In one teaching situation, I met a young man that appeared so heavily medicated that he had been rendered dysfunctional. He was lethargic. He walked as if he were in a stupor of sorts. His mother explained that he was extremely active and fidgety and consequently his grades suffered. She was reassuring, “He has Attention Deficit Disorder.”

Certainly, the prescription had not been the consequence of some malaise. The young man in his medicated condition was exhibiting enough of that. He did reasonably understand the subject material of the course he was in and he did manage satisfactory scores on exams but he seemed always to be in a daze often staring and with a kind of blank look about him.

The mother claimed to have no choice. Maybe she was right and maybe not.

Contrary to the mother’s opinion, was the medication given as an outcome of some relentless curiosity, some insatiable interest?

On a whim, I once applied for the principal’s job at a small private elementary school.

During the interview with the trustees, a board member asked, “Give a synopsis of your views on how you would discipline the children.”

I replied to her, “I would follow the prescriptions provided in the policy manual.”

Unaware, this board member was not asking for my comments on discipline that appears to be an inclination of purpose residing within the “heart” of a person. She mistakenly wanted to know my policy on rewards and punishments.

Albeit inadvertent, it is common. The notion of rewards and

punishments is incorrectly assumed to be the equivalent of discipline, a unique self-management quality.

From the dialog, this board member seemed to be searching for outside agencies to provide for the development of character she desired in her children but was unable to nurture.

In effect was she unknowingly searching for a solution to perhaps bothersome and annoying curiosity displayed by her child that instead should have been encouraged? Then do parents sometimes submit their children for medication because of natural but inconvenient and vexing behaviors that they do not understand?

Within a few days after the interview with the elementary school board of trustees, I had been called to meet with another smaller group more closely involved in the selection process. Nonetheless, I decided to withdraw from the proceedings leading to the job of principal. It was evident that I could not be for the board what at least one had wanted, someone managing children to fit into preconceived compartments as if the wonder of their future was foreseen as if the children needed to be channeled by some design into a narrow space hued by destiny itself.

I thought, "Could anyone assume the audacity to impose restrictions on learning by confining pliable minds to behavioral limits?

"On the contrary, school should be about nurturing wholesomeness."

Self-Management is a disposition toward persistent upgrading. Though it is personal, it is in line with the quality control principles of W. Edwards Deming and the manufacturing bottom line of Japan's "kaizen" that takes advantage of a continuum of small steady improvements. The thrust is to make progress in a direction of perfection and then to hold on to the gains. Many individuals have the desire for the attainment of goals and their beneficial outcomes but fail in their perseverance to achieve them.

The story of a little swimmer epitomizes the power of unyielding strong minded fortitude and willpower. This fifteen-year old high school sophomore asked the swim team coach for an opportunity. She was physically fit because she was a competitive gymnast but she was at best a novice in swimming. She only could offer the coach the assurance of commitment and dedication. With that, she earned his consent. She was on the team.

During training, her place was in the slow lane of the pool. That was not bothersome. It was exactly where she knew that she needed to be. Her immediate goal was to become good enough to be able to swim in the next fastest lane. Her stroke in the water was weak and her starts as well as her flip turns were poor. She worked diligently. She accepted every suggestion for improvement and welcomed every opportunity to swim.

Practice was not limited to the season. She worked throughout the year and during the summer especially. Videotapes helped her identify and correct flaws. Watching the tapes of champions gave her new insights into techniques. As skills improved, faster times were achieved. The stamina to swim longer distances increased. She was not a gifted swimmer. Her petite stature was limiting. Nonetheless, against these shortcomings she persisted practicing and improving day after day.

Each improvement was marked with reinforcing mental

celebrations. "I did it" served to reassure an "I can do it" mindset.

She moved into faster practice lanes and advanced to more competitive team positions. Soon she was swimming in events that determined team success. By the start of her third year in competitive swimming, she was voted team tri-captain.

Throughout the season, her performance in each event improved but her individual performance ended up just short of qualifying for the state finals. Nonetheless, she did earn a spot on the "four by one hundred yard" relay team. The team did not medal but her effort as the anchor swimmer was noticed. Her teammates and coach honored her with the "Most Improved Swimmer" award.

Her reply, "This is the greatest recognition I could have received, better than winning at state."

The award was not a multi-million dollar accomplishment. The world did not know but she knew and those on her team knew. It meant that effort and commitment to a goal had paid off. The achievement was not equal to the adversity that is faced by individuals with a debilitating illness or the challenges faced during the recovery from severe injuries. She really did not face overwhelming odds. She could have quit at any time. But, it was an achievement in day-to-day living. It was an achievement wrought from the fabric common to all. It was an accomplishment founded in basic character that grew from self-cultivated desire, undaunted will, and uncompromising resolve. It brought the enhancement of self-worth. It reinforced self-belief.

As a result, this young lady had established the personal wherewithal to set aside whatever may have been negative, to focus on the positive, and to work on developing the habit of confidence.

Goethe once wrote,

> Until one is committed, there is hesitancy, the chance to draw back . . . [but] the moment one

> definitely commits oneself, then Providence moves, too . . . A whole stream of events issues from the decision . . . which no man could have dreamed would have come his way.

In addition to the development of a worthy self-image and the structure for self-management, students need to develop certain personal attributes that are essential foundations for their self-development, employment worthiness, and leadership potential. Among these are: fundamental or basic knowledge, responsibility for actions, desire to attain worthy goals, courage to persist in the face of limiting challenges, and enthusiasm to continue despite setbacks.

While many students may develop these skills, why do some "lose heart" and give up their pursuit? When do they learn the phrase, "I can't and then begin to believe it?" When do they learn to "duck and hide" in the classroom and perhaps later in society to avoid involvement and participation masking the embarrassment of inability?

Does this begin at home even before school begins? What are the conditions of functionality that enable some students to know that shortfalls are likely momentary and certainly not a reflection on self-worth? What may cause some students to feel and believe that shortcomings must be avoided even though setbacks often clear and pave rather than litter and clutter the trail to success?

Everyone in the marketplace needs to have developed positive social interactive skills that incorporate at least a touch of reverence.

Once in an attempt to encourage students to adopt pleasant and cooperative skills, I wrote a thought for the day on the marker board, "People usually do not care about where you come from or what you look like. They do care about how you behave."

How is it that some youngsters develop unworkable relationships while others are cooperative? Are the roots founded in early childhood experiences? What influences have a significant lasting impact? Is it from the home, the school, or both? Could it be from some other cause or causes? Can defined interventions set aside these limiting influences? What would have to be done?

Apparently, individuals at an early age need to replace at least a touch of "I'm important" arrogance with a get along disposition. They need to adopt tolerance and wholesomeness in their thinking. Too often, youngsters develop self-destructive dispositions. Perhaps instinctively, they tend to exert their assumed importance upon others. The demeanor only leads to conflict with the curtailment of personal and economic productivity. On the other hand, working with a positive presence, a shared equality, and an optimistic outlook permits capitalization with opportunity.

Furthermore, success in the marketplace requires enthusiasm that drives persistence in action. Individuals need to be convinced that any achievement requires both the desire and the courage to pursue noble goals. They need to accept that the humility to assume responsibility for all actions taken and imposed is essential. Without humility, only denial is possible.

Encouraging rather than demanding and rewarding rather than depriving are foundation behaviors for communities, parents, teachers, and schools. These are dispositions that have been written about over the ages. They make good business sense in the marketplace because people want to be noticed for their accomplishments. They need to be patient with those who do not notice them as they should and when it is their time, they should enrich the environment with positive elements. It needs to be recognized that very early on and throughout school individuals incorporate these tools into their lifestyles.

The "Principle of Variation" assures that the more people that may be gathered together the more likely the group will include small to great differences rather than be all alike.

So, in teaching, what are the chances when a class is assembled its members will be alike?

The odds are against it; reliably, the larger a group the more likelihood of variety within. Individual faces as they are do not disclose the diversity nor do they provide any insight about the emotional structure and the nature of their dispositions.

With this in mind, the more students in a class, the greater will be the probability of a prohibitive and frustrating mixture that makes teaching most difficult, difficult in meeting individual needs and in treating individuals in familiar as well as common ways. With large classes, teaching and learning can become limited if not virtually impossible.

Of course, the opposite may be true. Some large groups of individuals can be docile and receptive.

While diversity fortunately adds to wholesomeness within a society, can an array of various compatible and conflicting differences in the classroom be managed simultaneously? How does each individual get served well?

In reply, it is sometimes convenient to compare teachers with individuals in the building trades and compare students with golfers.

If construction materials come to builders as students to teachers, the mixture would be extraordinary. The expectancy of usefulness might be unusual. Structures might be constructed with some degree of deficiency. Some structures might be attempted using only brick and stone with the omission of other essential materials. The challenge might be to build the Empire State Building, National Cathedral, or Golden Gate Bridge using wood alone. It cannot be done. In addition, a mix of other materials would be required. But, from wood, perhaps a stately house, covered bridge, or railed footpath could be superbly constructed.

The skyscraper, church, and overpass would at least require stone, glass, concrete, bricks, mortar, plastic, and steel. For the assembly of these a builder would require a division of labor, an array of specialist craftsmen each doing what it is they are good at not hampered by such unreasonable expectations that might require a plumber for example to assemble and install a drive track on a draw bridge. Yet the expectations of teachers are no less comparable.

Some students come as perhaps both bricks and mortar, others as steel and cement, while others maybe a mixture of stone, plastic, and glass. Just as if the same, the aggregation as it is must be shaped into "ideal" all-alike structures determined by sets of recognized though less than perfect guidelines.

Accordingly, sameness is expected. All students are expected to correctly answer the same questions. However, practically and functionally diversity is what is needed. Observations of nature confirm that. Indisputably, a field of weeds has a greater chance of survival than a golf course putting green composed only of ultra dwarf Bermuda grass.

To achieve what must be accomplished rather than what is sought by standards, a teacher, so to say, has to be a "jack of all trades" and ideally a master of most if not of each technique and strategy without recourse to some kind of all enabling alchemy that during the processes of teaching changes individuals into some homogeneous pliable and manageable conglomerate that then can be configured and restored as unique and purposeful with all of the beginning inventive, creative, imaginative, and innovative features. Realistically, what is expected to occur in a classroom is unparalleled compared with whatever can be done in most every other endeavor.

Classroom transmutation does not exist. Yet confronted, teachers have to find ways to simultaneously work with and preserve the individual differences the collection of all those variable qualities that are held dear that augment the merits of the diversity each individual brings. Each individual must be raised to their highest potential as if it were studded with inclusions, gilded with sparkle, and decorated with ornaments defined, dictated, and prescribed by a list of generally flawed standards. Now do that. Try!

In practicality, teachers, hopefully at their best, rather than some lackluster pile of rubble that serves little purpose render some kind of praiseworthy configuration with the assortment of constituents each retaining a distinctive blend but hopefully now augmented identifiable qualities.

Clearly, for the benefit of all, students must maintain their distinctiveness within a gathering of other unique individuals yet be raised to higher and higher levels of perfection as each component is in a marvelous building, the totality being greater than all of the assembled parts.

Now, what if a builder were given all kinds of materials, every conceivable kind but always each with some range of defects as knots and knotholes in wood, rust and dents on steel, chips and dings on bricks and stone? What if a builder would be asked to simultaneously form these flawed materials maximizing each quality into the most magnificent and utilitarian structure imaginable? How difficult would that be?

Instead, what if a teacher were asked to bring every student to some prescribed lofty level of perfection? What if that teacher were given twenty-four or even thirty-two teenaged individuals each with unique and wonderful qualities tempered with a variety of flaws and defects coupled with the exceptional variable of resiliency and the awesome power of refusal? What is it that this teacher could be expected to accomplish with such a particular assembly serving each to its maximum?

Golfers recognize that a specific style of play determined by individual qualities is more suitable for some courses but not so for others. Some golfers are more likely to win on some courses rather than on others.

What if an assigned task requires right-handedness rather than left-handedness? What do the "lefties" do? What if this demand persists day in and day out? How might attitudes be affected? What happens if some day in the future left-handedness is suddenly favored? Do all of the "lefties" immediately and wholeheartedly respond with expressions of joy and whooopeee? Can anyone predict what will occur? Which individuals will and which will not positively respond to the change?

In classrooms, many more variables exist and to satisfy every individual simultaneously is with certainty impossible. Expecting the patience that would be required by those students immediately unsatisfied is unrealistic.

How long will those have to endure in a given state before their moment arrives? How long can "lefthanders" languish in a "right-handed" environment when in reality they are endowed as "left-handed" individuals? Would they be able to immediately recognize a change should it occur? Then, how would each respond should their moment arrive with enthusiasm or indifference? Have some grown tired from waiting?

Presumably, are building materials in a construction yard each "waiting" to be used while deteriorating and wasting away from disuse? Are outcomes determined by the preferences of the teacher that chance has interrelated?

An unimaginable spectrum of possibilities as well as difficulties arises in the form of who, what, when, how, and so on!

When all else fails, teachers do what teachers have always done out of necessity, literally they build what they know how to build.

For the sake of example, some may be well versed in the building of birdhouses. These will try to build birdhouses out of everything that comes their way. Others may have strengths in putting together fireplaces. Expect that these will try to put together fireplaces out of everything they get. Each will assemble what they are good at constructing. Some good at birdhouses given bricks and mortar may though unrealistically try to construct birdhouses using the bricks and mortar.

Is it possible that fine grain wood suitable for carvings might end up as birdhouses more or less? Will the wood be ruined?

Well, not exactly but the precious wood might have been shaped for an alternative perhaps more suitable use. The overriding important thing is that the finished product should have the appropriate amounts and kinds of twinkle, tinsel, and glitter.

The questions are: Will it? Does it? Is it at its best? Is it at all possible? What determines which material will be used and when?

Well, it is relatively easy. Resort to sorting and grouping the so to say materials so that each will be used to its maximum. In schools, this is accomplished in a fashion through testing. But, please! Each individual in school is not at all like a brick or a marble cornerstone, an “I” beam or a rail, a fine grain walnut or mahogany piece with some rather specific significance. Each individual is a person with enormous combinations of many, many interacting and cross influencing characteristics and qualities with rudimentary formations occurring even before birth.

What if after the most thorough definitive testing, students are put into somewhat homogeneous but nonetheless heterogeneous groups? Is this ideal? What if the teacher so to say is left-handed and the students in the group are essentially right-handed? Figuratively, what if the teacher has an inclination for working with glass rather than plastic?

Surely, the teacher could form a beautiful vase from the one and be frustrated in the utilization of the other. It seems that testing students for skills as well as performance levels coupled with personality indicators is not the answer. But, that is all there is. Likewise, the analytical qualification of teachers is not the answer.

Wherein may be the ideal? In any given school is it possible let alone realistic to expect to ideally and uniquely mix and match every student and teacher to maximize outcomes?

If it happens, it is likely to be a quirk, atypical and rare.

With some insight it is possible to set up a learning environment that does come closer to the ideal than may appear. Publisher put together textbooks in conjunction with shadow writers that are certainly lobbied into adoption for general use as if one size fits all need to be set aside permitting the optimization of potential. Schools do need to be restructured with the master teacher and associates responsible for the activities that translate into maximized learning focused upon individualized instruction systems.

The method ideally suited for the diversity among learners is the individualized format but over the years instruction so designed seems to have gone missing. While this wonderful opportunity in education seems to have slipped away some hope remains for its rebirth.

With the emergence of the internet, with an obvious need for convenience, an indifferent form of individualized instruction has emerged obliquely absorbed into the fabric of distance education and other on-line access programs. However, overlooked in this impersonal format are the worthy merits and benefits of a powerful system of carefully selected and evaluated tools, an individualized system enabling efficient and effective learning.

35

After returning to the profession of high school science teacher interrupted by a rather long absence, thirty years give or take one or two, I felt compelled to write my thoughts about schools and students.

Retired from industry, sitting on the porch would not be an option. Trusting my inclinations, the wherewithal to be a successful teacher as once I had been was still present.

When asked why I decided to get back to what had seemed to be my life's calling, the response was simple, "To help kids learn."

"Beware," I was told by well meaning friends.

Supposedly, much had changed.

They warned, "You will find the students to be different in many ways: less restrained and even unruly; more talkative, acidic, impulsive; dressing boldly as if to make a statement; lacking in regard; and short in overall respect."

I thought, "I can do this. I can make a difference. What can be so prohibitive?"

Eventually, I would concede to some of my advice givers that the teaching load had increased measurably: extended class periods and lengthened school calendar including added time consuming responsibilities and duties by requirement "volunteering" for outdoor supervision assuring acceptable parking lot behavior plus hallway oversight maintaining order while students wandered to and fro at the beginning and end of the school day. Combined, these extra contributions would use up over fifty hours during the course of an academic year. This coupled with meetings and professional development obligations would be prohibitive. None of these deemed necessary add-on demands is teaching which had been my singular interest. I would deal with it.

Overall, the students that I worked with were substantively the same as those that I encountered years ago maybe a different blend more burdened with complex needs influenced by their generously provocative environment. Those with high aspirations could be found among them.

In contrast were the more than few less fortunate fundamentally clueless without a goal and deficient in desire lacking in ambition to attain a measure of success. These students were indeed outwardly obnoxious and confrontational but as I met with them over time, some would acquiesce giving up at least a thin slice of their need to display a revolting behavioral manner.

I would evolve to admit that early on in my teaching years when my assignments also required working with troubled maturing teenagers, those students then did seem to be a bit more compliant and cooperative, less obstinate, more inclined to try.

As had been presumed, most of the students were open to guidance. These, with some variance, accepted themselves as "okay" within their context living in the present with personal insecurities perhaps testing their environment. Regrettably, in one aspect, they were conspicuous with little regard for or awareness of consequences. Maybe this characteristic ever present heretofore had gone unnoticed. Its recognition appears to deserve some future reflection.

When a novice, well, a young teacher, I had been assigned the management of a study hall jammed with one hundred and twenty students. Literally, they were in the hall, four rows wide with an aisle between each row and thirty desks in length on the uppermost third floor of the school building. Every day, the students from all walks of life and all levels of income studied quietly only occasionally a few might put their heads down to rest. Undisturbed, I would read a weekly business newspaper.

Given an across the board mix, even getting along reasonably well with most students, the workable gathering of one hundred or more of this generation as I have encountered would be impossible conceivably chaotic because of only those few who might impose themselves having succumb to a less restrained unaccommodating behavior style demonstrating personal discipline shortfalls a likely consequence of the trauma of regrettable experiences and the rigors of ill advised training. Those exceptionally disruptive individuals in all probability would impose their identity crisis as if to say, "Do you know who I am? I'm here! I need recognition." Protected by mandates, their wounded being would certainly prohibit the potential development of the worthy majority.

While essentially amenable, many of the students that I had met during these last few years seemed to be unwilling to make good use of available class time. Possibly they do not know how. They do not comprehend the value of opportunity. They commonly say, "I would rather study and do my work at home." Of course, that did not happen. With their universal reply, they may have been saying something that has yet to be heard. It just may be a protective veneer masking a deficiency in self-management.

Moreover, I did find the public school environment emphatically regimented, secured with hallway cameras, and reinforced with the presence of police officers certainly attempting to influence the misguided boisterous groups purposefully volatile in their disposition, aimless in their pursuits likely focused upon the trivial.

From time to time student fistfights did occur involving the boys. The girls were not immune. Outbreaks in and around the school were not atypical. Such incidents did occur during my early school days. Obviously, all students cannot be regarded as gentlemen and ladies. Unfortunately, on the second day of the public school assignment that I accepted, I had to intervene separating two girls in a hallway hair pulling slugfest. Later in that term, I had to deal with two boys in a roll about the classroom rumble toppling desks at the onset of a laboratory activity. That was frightening. Of course, both are events to remember, moments in a day's work. Indeed.

Perhaps today, more students appear as socially disabled but any in depth comparison or detailed analysis may be without justification, maybe pointless without a comparison group. The challenge is to work in the present environment with the next generation of adults leading them as they are to higher order achievement.

On my way to work one morning engrossed in anticipation, I thought, "Oh my, No Child Left Behind, this can never work. It is a great slogan how can anyone not embrace all that it signifies? Yet, it is so misleading. While an ideal, it is truly a slight of hand."

Though we push hard to leave no child behind, we tend to leave all behind because of structure rigidity. Standards, syllabi, and textbooks with collaterals are in effect increasing illiteracy within the system.

These impositions cannot work rendering enhancement or enrichment because while on paper all looks good, the standards are curtailing the diversity of individuality and they are stimulating divisiveness to measure up. Rather than teaching to achieve purposeful ideals and commendable derivatives, all is necessarily test driven. The focus is riveted on the test score. It has become all that matters with certainty.

The test results will show improvement one way or another but really the real test is in the enabled marketplace-ready individual making a contribution.

With the implementation of standards, the range for learning is now as narrow as the standards will allow. The learning that is most productive and elevating, the most needed in the fulfillment of every individual, has become restricted. While the intention was noble, to have everyone at least minimally educated, all will be schooled to achieve only that minimum. The highest expectation has become the bottom line. The diversity that is required for a wholesome society certainly will be lost.

The youngsters, the teenagers, the students of our day are worth so much more than anything the standards can bring. As the standards are achieved only the standard setters will be able to revel in satisfaction and self-gratification.

I can hear it, "Behold what we have accomplished. Every school is achieving at least at the established level. They measured up to our standards. They have succeeded to our expectations."

In contrast, I am inclined to say, "Too bad, for those students, for all of us. Surely, they could have accomplished so much more. We would be so much better off otherwise."

During the 1980's, the "commanding heights" industries were deregulated for the good of all. Free markets were seen as the way to go. The market would eventually stabilize itself according to the economic principles of Friedrich Hayek and Milton Friedman.

In considering that, should schools be permitted to function under the same free market principles? Unconfined, without prohibitive congestion, rules, and regulations, could schools rise above as well as develop and evolve as they must? Do we not trust ourselves?

As American society had overcome conflict and adversity and as imagination had inspired inventiveness enabling wholesome lifestyles and adventure searching beyond the limits of our galaxy, we can with the same wherewithal educate our children. Improvements that are more than superficial will not come about because of a piece of legislation but rather by a challenge to ingenuity as eyes were once set upon landing on the moon.

Now, unfortunate as it is, students are inclined to be answer driven even those that do care about learning and advancing their status. For them, the major issue is, "What's the right answer."

"Why? What has happened over the years? What has led to this shortcoming in teaching and learning?"

I have come to believe that teachers in an attempt to "control" their classes have mistakenly taken advantage of all the "canned" materials that highly competitive publishers generate. The costs though hidden may be unaffordable. Unwittingly, teachers have surrendered their individuality and at a premium of course, their creativity as well. They have forfeited their uniqueness in the profession maybe because they have less professional time maybe because they are engaged in some kind of prescribed obligation like monitoring student behavior in the cafeteria.

Perhaps textbook adoptions should take place only as needed. Maybe teachers should write their own materials and textbooks. But, every five to ten years more or less, a new textbook must be selected from among the competitors. In that between adoptions time, what significant changes may have occurred except in science?

Then, all that seems needed is a textbook supplement of a few pages that within days can be released or a teacher prepared addendum would do. If something is essential, worth teaching, it needs to be introduced without delay. Always, the text materials would be up to date.

Who would need a new book?

Still, the sale of textbooks in the context of a rigid system must go on. The publisher stays in business, a necessity for the economy. As it is students may not be able to read about any new discoveries only those recorded in textbooks for maybe five or ten years.

Reliably, for every moment of every occasion, a worksheet can be found without meaningful substance. Nothing is unique and under development by a teacher to be implemented to determine its merits. On the contrary, file cabinets are filled with countless ready to go supplemental sheets, busy work for every conceivable occasion.

One may be inclined to say, "At least the students are busy with something and if busy, classroom difficulties are minimized."

But, are the students learning anything by copying a word or two onto a line, a textbook sighting that has value only in the hunt?

Reading does not take place as proposed by the "reading guides." Rather "word search" is the consequent activity.

This form of "limited pursuit for the answer" must stop.

In addition, I have come to realize that much of what teachers were doing years ago as part of their work is being re-implemented as if the discoveries were as recent as perhaps, yesterday. For example, data analysis methods and instructional presentation skills and techniques are being offered as a method of school improvement.

How did this past practice ever fall by the wayside?

The methods of internal assessment should have been ever present supporting the most needed on going and continuous classroom improvement.

I think, "If re-inventing and re-adopting are the trend, then the need to go back and resurrect much more of what was commonplace is overriding and must be fitted into the array of available technology. This would serve the purpose of individualizing the instructional methods that might enable real growth and learning. Positive interaction between teacher and student would become more likely, productive and rewarding.

Serious consideration needs to be given to what schools should be about and the impact of the various requirements and responsibilities. In a free enterprise society, schools have become over regulated. Every incident is an excuse that enables tightening the grip. Outside accrediting agencies are at best only indirectly helpful. Most of what they require seems to be a paper shuffle.

Monitors and observers enter. Administrators respond with a proposal for improvement. Documents are generated. Later, somehow certification is achieved. The administration is relieved.

The teachers are praised and thanked for their effort and cooperation. The board is pleased. The public is informed. It seems like such serious business but in effect, it is highly superficial. The last event in the sequence is, "File it."

In their own right, schools should become learning organizations and lead the way. This is only possible if individual schools are restructured totally linked to an internal common goal embracing core values all pulling in the same direction with each individual component reinforcing the efforts of the others helping students learn efficiently and effectively. Teachers could then conduct personal research that then could be published and shared through in-house produced periodicals available to others in the profession and the public as well. That would be so wonderful.

In the global marketplace, astronauts 220 miles above the earth traveling at more or less 24,000 miles per hour are working in space repairing their vehicle. This is absolutely marvelous and how spectacular it must be to look over your shoulder to see the earth, moon, and other entities of the universe.

On the other hand, infants and children as well as adults are starving in various parts of the world. Too weak to shoo them away, flies are everywhere on their faces, in their noses and ears, laying their eggs. Is the scene tragically pathetic?

The Amazon forest is being destroyed, reefs are being destroyed, productivity of the oceans is in decline, and glaciers are melting. What else is new?

Others out of pure hatred are blowing people up in buildings and subways as well along roadways. Why? What good can be derived from such destruction? Can these actions and motivations ever be understood?

What does it take to become Good Citizens of Earth?

That is the question before us. The elements that are needed can only be put into place in the context of our schools. This opportunity to teach, to help the children of our time must not slip away.

The children including teenagers in schools need to get out into the world and learn to live in it. They need to talk with the ordinary people, the man on the street, and record their stories. They need to go on field trips that introduce them to the work and experiences of those around them. They need to discover. And, perhaps on a rainy day, they need to just watch the falling drops as the clouds roll by and even search for a rainbow that just might appear. They need to wonder. A lot is riding on the outcome of their education. For anything short of good, the cost to each and everyone is too great.

On my first day back in a school building, two days before classes would begin filled with anticipation of students in the process of opening the door to the classroom that had been assigned, I looked up to see a young lady with books in her arms and her friend walking along presumably en route to her locker. Instead, because she had noticed me, she changed her direction to present herself.

She was petite with a special kind of energy and alertness. You would fall short in describing her as enthusiastic. Her face was cheerful. Her eyes sparkled with delight. Her smile conveyed a heart-centered happiness. She said, “Hi! Are you Dr. Dyman?”

“Yes.” I answered somewhat taken by surprise that anyone would know my name.

She continued, “I’m Lindsay and this is my friend with me for the day. You’re gonna be my teacher. I’m in your environmental science class right here in this room.”

Looking to her, I began to smile.

She went on, “Yes, I’m looking forward to it. And, welcome to my school.”

I replied, "Thank you. I'm looking forward to being here and to working you."

With eyes now gleaming, she said, "I have to put my books in my locker. And, I'll see you in a couple of days. Once again, welcome."

"Yes, bye for now," I answered.

Lindsay attended class only occasionally. She had leukemia. She died during that school year. And, when I pray, I often think of her reflecting on her delightfulness and elatedness.

She was the first and only one who had welcomed me back to what had been my life for so many years. That moment gave me the assurance that overcame my doubts. The classroom is where I do belong and my mission is unchanged, to help the young men and women of this day to learn to be Good Citizens of Earth.

Re-entry had not been easy. The work had been difficult, demanding, and draining. Hopefully, the outcomes of my effort will be priceless. Some have said that.

I keep in my mind a quote from *The Diary of Anne Frank*.

> Each day, I try to be what I'd like to be if there were
> no people to keep me from doing so.

Three days after writing this her hiding place was discovered. Anne Frank was sent to the Bergen-Belsen concentration camp. There, before she was fifteen years old, she died.

Each day everyone should be given every opportunity to be all that they can be especially those still in school. Remember, more than they need us, we need them.

NOTES

Schools
- are too big
- need to become learning organizations
- should provide individualized instruction
- develop a set of core values
- abandon homework for its own sake
- ought to become self-accountable
- provide for research studies and publication vehicles
- enable students to move on as prepared

Students must
- maintain curiosity
- structure positive dispositions
- learn to study
- establish the skill of listening
- get more rest and relaxation for their number one job
- enjoy a nurturing environment free from fear

Principals
- have to be replaced with a master teacher concept
  managing interactive instructional programs

Teachers
- have to adopt self-accountability measures for the
  improvement of instructional presentations
- have to be dedicated to caring

Communities
- have to achieve the wealth that enables best practices
  helping their children acquire the qualities to be
  Good Citizens of Earth.

www.ingramcontent.com/pod-product-compliance
Ingram Content Group UK Ltd.
Pitfield, Milton Keynes, MK11 3LW, UK
UKHW020144250726
13967UKWH00002B/864